AF415350

Hellbound: Hellraiser Ii

Howard Mahmood

FADE IN:

TITLES

The screen is composed of large, straight-edge areas of black and white that rest against each other in a manner that suggests some kind of pattern, without making a final sense; it is as if we are too close to something that, could we see it from a distance, would be clear to us.

These areas shift and change - both their own shape and their relationship to their neighbors. New patterns are being made, new solutions found - but they are just beyond our comprehension.

The effect should be aesthetically pleasing but simultaneously frustrating and, perhaps, a little unsettling.

Shortly into this sequence, and subsequently inter-cut throughout, we begin to see, in FLASHBACK, the story of

HELLRAISER. Arriving first as very short shock-images, these brief sections eventually convey to the audience all the necessary emotional and narrative information they will need to understand the background to HELLBOUND.

Meanwhile, the black and white shapes are still moving, the unseen patterns still shifting.

Over this constantly mobile background, the TITLES begin to appear.

As the TITLES unroll, another change comes over the puzzle pieces behind them. Where before they moved and related only in two dimensions, gradually we see that they are now claiming depth as well. The puzzle we are looking at is now a three-dimensional one. The pieces are now solid blocks of various geometric shapes, locking together, moving apart, finding their final position.

Finally, as the TITLES come to their conclusion, the camera pulls back until we can see clearly what we have been looking at. As the final piece clicks into positions we see it is THE LAMENT

CONFIGURATION from HELLRAISER.

The closed box rests before our eyes a moment and then the circle in the centre of the side that faces us gives way to an image of a dusty street with a market. Simultaneous to this, the camera

TRACKS into this image until it fills the screen

EXT A STREET BAZAAR DAY

The TRACK continues up through the market and then turns through the stalls to find a store behind them. As we TRACK through the store's doorway, we pass through a beaded curtain that momentarily reminds us of the TORTURE ROOM in HELLRAISER.

INT. STORE DAY

Once we are in the store itself, though, this impression disappears.

It is an ordinary, slightly seedy, junk shop.

The stall seems to sell an odd mixture of items; native trinkets share space with second-hand items from European colonists. These second-hand goods give us some sense of period. They suggest the late 'twenties/early 'thirties. This is reinforced by the sounds coming from one of them, an old-fashioned mahogany-cased wireless. A foreign voice speaks from it in a language we don't understand, though perhaps the words "BBC world service" are discerned in the middle, and then a dance-hall tune of the period begins to play. (Depending on availability, it would be nice to have something relevant - 'I'll follow my Secret Heart', perhaps, or 'Dancing in the Dark'.)

Into shot comes an ENGLISH OFFICER. His uniform, too, suggests the 'twenties, the last days of Empire. He is tall, thin, and dark-haired, but at no stage do we see his face clearly. He stands in front of the stall.

The TRADER suddenly stands behind the counter. He has been crouched beneath it, as if checking or preparing something. He is a big, impressive-looking black man. His face is totally impassive as he stares at his customer.

Neither of the men speak. Obviously, a deal has already been struck and today is the pay-off.

The OFFICER, a little arrogantly - suggesting racist contempt, slaps down a bag of gold on the stall's counter.

Keeping his eyes firmly on the OFFICER, he reaches beneath him and brings something up from under the counter and places it In the OFFICER'S outstretched hand. He is holding a LAMENT

CONFIGURATION.

The OFFICER turns and leaves. The camera TRACKS out of the store, looking at the TRADER as he watches the departing OFFICER.

INT THE OFFICER'S QUANSETT HUT DAY

It is typical of temporary military quarters, complete with a curved ceiling of corrugated material. It is stripped of furniture.

The blinds are down.

The OFFICER, still in uniform, sits cross-legged, the BOX held before him.

He is already well into the solving process and very soon after the shot begins the BOX begins to speed its own solution.

Finally, two sections of the BOX shoot upwards and begin to peel apart from each other, ready to reveal its secret.

The OFFICER, suddenly nervous, drops the BOX and scuttles back across the floor to stare at it. The BOX lands upright, its extended parts still open above it. For a beat of two, nothing happens. We become aware of the OFFICER'S pulse, throbbing excitedly on the soundtrack.

INT THE OFFICER'S QUANSETT HUT DAY OFFICER'S P.O.V.

Slowly we, the camera, and the OFFICER, move towards the still, silent, but menacing BOX.

We approach it until finally we are above it, looking down into the opening it has made in itself. There is undefined movement inside.

Suddenly, something flies up directly at us. We glimpse it only briefly, but enough to see its nature. Unlike the hooks that flaw at FRANK in HELLRAISER, this is more organic than metallic.

Pink and flesh-like but on a long gray-blue stalk, it flies upward, its lips peeling apart gapingly to reveal scores of yellow, discoloured, and viciously sharp teeth-like hooks.

The OFFICER screams and the screen begins to take on a red tint so that, just as the thing is about to fill the screen with its hungry mouth, the entire screen turns red.
The red screen is held for a second and then suddenly becomes complete blackness.

INT BLACK SPACE
The black screen continues and, rising slowly from it and falling back slowly into it, in a dream-like, surrealistic manner, come various images of the OFFICER'S torment/pleasure in Hell.
By various camera tricks, such as step-printing or optical blurring, his face is still not clearly seen, but is seen enough for us to see his sensual, almost orgasmic responses to what is being done to him.
Cuts appear spontaneously across his face, leaving a grid like crisscross pattern of wounds.
Finally, a disembodied hand gripping a hammer drives nails into each corner formed by these wounds and, as the face comes into full view for the first time, we realize who this is. It is PINHEAD from HELLRAISER. PINHEAD'S completed face floats on the blackness and stares out at us.

PINHEAD
(echoed & slow)
Kirsty, come to daddy
The tiny silence following PINHEAD's words is shattered by a piercing and terrified scream.

INT HOSPITAL ROOM NIGHT
The scream continues, but the blackness is replaced by KIRSTY's anguished face; it is she who is screaming. The scream subsides, replaced by breathless panting accompanied by rapid eye movement.

RONSON
(off camera)
Ah, you're awake. Good.
We pull out to see that KIRSTY is sitting up, fully dressed, on a hospital bed. RONSON, a police detective, sits on a plain wooden chair, which is the only other piece of furniture in the room.
The walls are bare save for a piece of primitive art on one wall, and, on another, a circular barred window looking out.
RONSON stands up and walks to the foot of the bed. He rests his hand on the bed's metal frame and smiles a perfunctory smile.

RONSON
Tell you what - we'll make a deal. I'll tell you what I know, then you tell me what you know. O.K.?
KIRSTY is still re-orienting herself. She blinks a few times and then focuses on RONSON's hands gripping the bed.

RONSON
O.K.?
KIRSTY looks up at RONSON's face and then around at the room.

KIRSTY
Where am I?

RONSON
You're in the Malahide Institute.
It's a psychiatric hospital. But, hey, don't feel judged - it was just the nearest place to
bring you.
Remember? You and your boyfriend... ?

KIRSTY
Steve...

RONSON
Don't worry. He's O.K. We sent him home hours ago. Jeez, what a story.
He puts a cigarette in his mouth and lights it.

RONSON
What was it, kid? Smack? Angel dust?
Don't tell me acid's back in fashion?

KIRSTY
What are you talking about? Who are you?

RONSON
Oh, excuse me...
RONSON reaches in his jacket and flashes an I.D.

RONSON
Ronson. Homicide. I'm this district's slash and dash expert.
Made a career of the nasty ones.
That's why I was at your
Dad's house. Jesus, what a mess.
KIRSTY'S eyes prick with tears. She looks away from RONSON.
KIRSTY (to herself)
Daddy...

INT JUNK ROOM LODOVICO STREET NIGHT
CORTEZ, a POLICE OFFICER, shifts some unpacked crates to allow a closer look at
the shriveled and deformed corpse of one of FRANK and JULIA'S victims.

CORTEZ
Jesus...

CORTEZ prods at the corpse with his night-stick, attempting to turn it over. A stream of maggots pours from the mouth and the cavity that used to be its throat.
CORTEZ jumps back in disgust and knocks against one of the several wardrobes in the cluttered room. Another corpse flies out at him, as decayed and flvblown as the first.
CORTEZ draws his gun and empties it blowing the corpses head off, scattering flesh, mucus, and bone - but no blood - everywhere before realizing it is already dead.
He realises what he has done and lowers his weapon sheepishly.

CORTEZ
Oh. shit...

INT. HOSPITAL ROOM DAY
RONSON is sitting back in the chair, looking at the now slightly calmer KIRSTY.

RONSON
We got two missing people and a house full of corpses.
He holds out his hand towards KIRSTY in a theatrical manner.

RONSON
Talk to me.
KIRSTY swings her legs off the bad, but remains sitting on it, her feet on the floor. She doesn't look directly at RONSON but begins to take in the (few) details of the room for the first time.

KIRSTY
I thought Steve had talked to you?

RONSON
Oh, pardon me. I obviously didn't convey my hesitation to take his story at face-value.
No, YOU talk to me. But - do me a favor? - none of this DEMONS crap.
KIRSTY closes her eyes, almost wincing, as memory comes.
KIRSTY opens her eyes. Consciously, she slows the rhythm of the dialogue down.

KIRSTY
He talked about Demons, huh?

RONSON
Yeah.
KIRSTY turns her head to look directly at RONSON.

KIRSTY
It's true. All of it. It's all true.
RONSON stares at her, impressed by her conviction and intensity.
There is a second of shared silence.
Suddenly, a shocking ELECTRONIC CRACKLE shatters the mood. RONSON starts, then realises it is the radio at his belt. He snatches it up and speaks into it.

RONSON
Ronson.

INT BEDROOM LODOVICO STREET NIGHT
Another OFFICER, KUCICH, is standing, radio in hand, by the blood-stained mattress.
CORTEZ stands beside him, gun now safely re-holstered.

KUCICH

Kucich here,sir. We just found another one, though it suffered a little...
KUCICH looks at CORTEZ, who looks embarrassed.

KUCICH

...er, accidental damage in discovery.
Anyway, just about the only portable evidence we've got here - apart from human remains - is the mattress. Looks like someone was messed up real bad on it.

INT HOSPITAL ROOM NIGHT
KUCICH
(off-camera)
Can we send it downtown?
RONSON throws KIRSTY a look of exasperation with his colleague.
The camera stays on KIRSTY's face as RONSON speaks.

RONSON
What the hell are you asking me for? Tag it. Move it.
KIRSTY (to herself)
The mattress... The mattress... JULIA.
Without waiting for a reply, RONSON switches the radio off and clips it back to his belt.

INT BEDROOM STREET NIGHT
We are looking at the mattress. KUCICH has left the room.
CORTEZ draws a pad from his packet. The pad is stapled, and the staple has been badly inserted and is not closed property.
In the act of tearing a label from the pad, CORTEZ catches his thumb on the staple.

OFFICER
Shit!
The label is adhesive-backed. CORTEZ licks it and presses it on the mattress. He writes on it - 55L/E1. As he stands up from doing this, a single drop of blood from his thumb lands on the mattress. (It is important that we see it is only a single drop - and nothing like the amount LARRY spilled on the floorboards.)
CORTEZ leaves the room to fetch a colleague to help him move the mattress. We move in to see the drop of blood disappear very quickly into the mattress, as if it is being sucked in.

As this happens, we hear on the soundtrack the faintest RUMBLE.

INT OPERATING ROOM NIGHT
A somewhat antiquated and frightening operating room, filled with machines, monitors, and surgical instruments. The corners of the room fall away to shadow.
Sitting upright in the centre of the room is a FEMALE PATIENT.
She is awake and staring out at the camera. Twin probes/clamps are in each of her ears to hold her in place. Her head is shaved and the skin on the back of her head has been cut open and peeled apart. The flaps of the skin are held away from the area being worked on by four clamps. (we never actually see round to the exposed brain itself)
Immediately behind her, and probing with professional skill and coolness into her exposed brain, is DOCTOR MALAHIDE. He is in his late forties and looks like all the great doctors look - rational, civilized, competent, and powerful. There is an intensity in his eyes and the lines of his face though that suggests something more than normal.
The room has several attentive listeners and observers, but the one nearest to MALAHIDE is his personal student/assistant KYLE
MACRAE, young, conventionally good-looking, with an open, friendly, face.
MALAHIDE is holding forth on the secrets of his trade, several times looking away from his patient while still working on her, to make sure his audience understand his points.

MALAHIDE
We can bring them back properly more often than scientific orthodoxy dictates, ladies and gentlemen. And the knife, far from the enemy of of analysis, is often its greatest ally in solving the puzzles of psychosis. Analysis isolates and massages. Surgery pinpoints and corrects. ... though you've got to know what you're doing, of course...
Polite laughter from several students.

MALAHIDE
Some things are obvious. Here, for example, ...
He prods in at a specific area.

MALAHIDE
...are the optical motor nerve control centers.
The PATIENT begins to blink in time with MALAHIDE'S prodding.
The affect is half-comical, half-distressing. Perhaps MALAHIDE carries it on just that half-second too long for innocent demonstration. But the students give impressed murmurs anyway.

MALAHIDE
Now. This case. A deeply-buried psychosis severe enough to produce frighteningly frequent hysteria and aggression. Incurable. Say others. Not so.
Analysis isolates. The knife exposes. Medication controls.
As he speaks, MALAHIDE injects a syringe directly into the
PATIENT's brain. Her face spasms momentarily.
MALAHIDE stands back slightly. His face is serene, calm, and confident.

He takes a small, motorised drill and sets to work on the brain.

MALAHIDE
And then, ladies and gentlemen, we
REBUILD. With all the care and knowledge that our years of training have given us ...
He looks around at them all, smiling slightly.

MALAHIDE
... WE BRING THEM BACK.
The students murmur their approval. Perhaps they even applaud.
MALAHIDE acknowledges their reaction with a modest nod.
Suddenly, an intercom on the wall cuts in.

INTERCOM
Dr. Malahide, the new arrival is awake, and appears very distressed.
MALAHIDE steps back briskly and begins to peel his cloves off.
He nods at a nearby student.

MALAHIDE
My part in this is over. You may tidy up for me. Kyle, you come with me.
MALAHIDE and KYLE leave the room.

INT HOSPITAL ROOM NIGHT
KIRSTY has her hands over her face and is shaking. RONSON stands and crosses to
her. He takes her hand from her face and calms her.

RONSON
Easy, easy. Whatever happened, whatever you saw, it's not here now.

KIRSTY
I saw it...him. But I got away.
And I took the box. And I solved it. And they came.

RONSON
Who?

KIRSTY
The Cenobites.
She stares directly at RONSON, daring him to disbelieve.

KIRSTY
The Demons.
RONSON stares back, perhaps a glimmer of belief in his eyes.
On the soundtrack, the sudden and shocking sound of a door being slammed open and
hitting the wall.
KIRSTY screams. Even RONSON is startled.

In the doorway are DOCTOR MALAHIDE and KYLE. MALAHIDE advances into the room, smiling apologetically as he does so.

MALAHIDE
Sorry. Must get that door fixed. Detective Ronson?
MALAHIDE holds his hand out, as RONSON nods in response.

MALAHIDE
I am Doctor Malahide.
The man shake hands. MALAHIDE gestures behind him.

MALAHIDE
My assistant, Kyle Macrae. And this must be Kirsty?
MALAHIDE speaks quickly, as if to get the formalities out of the way. As he says her name, he smiles benignly at KIRSTY who, still distraught from her memories and shocked at the slamming of the door, simply stares at him.
MALAHIDE turns his attention back to RONSON, drawing him away and speaking to him in a lower voice.
Meanwhile, KYLE walks over to KIRSTY and smiles at her - long enough to embarrass her into smiling back.

MALAHIDE
I've read the boy's statement.
Quite the adventure they believe they had. I'd like to talk to her alone. Do you think ... ?
RONSON looks over his shoulder at KIRSTY. He then looks carefully at MALAHIDE and then nods slowly.

RONSON
Mmmm. O.K. Frankly, I think she's more your territory than mine. Shame.
RONSON looks back at KIRSTY.

RONSON
Kirsty. Doctor Malahide's going to look after you now. Maybe we could talk some more tomorrow.
KIRSTY nods vaguely and then, just as RONSON reaches the door, calls out to him.

KIRSTY
Wait! The mattress. You've got to destroy it. She DIED on it, you see. The mattress. It's haunted now. She can come back... like Frank. SHE CAN COME BACK.
RONSON smiles helplessly at her, then glances at MALAHIDE with a
"you see what I mean" expression, and leaves the room.
KIRSTY (to herself)
The mattress ...
MALAHIDE stares at her briefly, with a strange expression on his face and then abruptly follows RONSON through the door.

KIRSTY is too absorbed to notice this odd behavior, but KYLE stares incredulously as MALAHIDE leaves the room.

KYLE
Uh...excuse me a moment.
He follows to the door and stands in the doorway, looking down the corridor.

INT HOSPITAL CORRIDOR NIGHT
RONSON stands before a set of double-doors, talking to a

UNIFORMED OFFICER.
MALAHIDE comes into view, walking swiftly, and instantly talks over their conversation.

MALAHIDE
Detective. I'll be able to help this girl. But I need your assistance ...

INT HOSPITAL CORRIDOR NIGHT
Looking back at the corridor, we see the door to KIRSTY'S room ajar, and KYLE standing by it looking down.

INT HOSPITAL CORRIDOR NIGHT (KYLE' P.O.V)
A LONG SHOT of MALAHIDE and RONSON. KYLE, and we, are too far away to hear what is said, but MALAHIDE in nodding and gesturing emphatically, as if persuading RONSON of something.

INT HOSPITAL ROOM NIGHT
KYLE returns into the room and closes the door. His expression is puzzled, troubled. Then he remembers there is a patient here and he smiles.

KYLE
So...You're Kirsty, huh?

KIRSTY
You a doctor, too?
KYLE smiles again.

KYLE
Nearly a doctor. I'm Kyle
Macrae. Call me Kyle.
KIRSTY draws a deep breath, temporarily calmed. She even manages a smile.

KIRSTY
Hi, Kyle.
MALAHIDE re-enters the room.

MALAHIDE
Now, Kirsty...
KIRSTY looks at him warily.

KIRSTY
The cop. He didn't believe me.

MALAHIDE
I suspect not. But that doesn't necessarily mean you're wrong, does it?

KIRSTY
Do you believe me?
MALAHIDE offers a re-assuring laugh.

MALAHIDE
Well, I don't know yet.
However, you're not lying.
YOU believe this is the truth.

KIRSTY
It IS the truth.
Suddenly, the door opens again. An INTERN is standing there. For the briefest of moments, MALAHIDE looks furious and then, catching himself, assumes his calm demeanor.

MALAHIDE
Well?

INTERN
Sorry, Dr. Malahide. But it's
Tiffany. She's escaped ... again.
MALAHIDE sighs.

MALAHIDE
Very Well.
He looks down at KIRSTY.

KIRSTY
I'm sorry, Kirsty. Kyle will come back with something to help you sleep. We shall speak tomorrow.
MALAHIDE and KYLE follow the intern from the room, KYLE giving a last friendly smile as the door closes behind them.

EXT. CARNIVAL NIGHT

We are staring down the midway of a deserted carnival. On either side, stalls and rides beckon to pleasures that their locked doors and tarpaulin-draped entrances deny. A light rain is falling.

A huge wooden cut-out of a grinning clown dominates one stall while the sign beneath him seems to state the ethos of the whole place; LOTS 'O' FUN.

Another has a banner proclaiming FREAK SHOW, with the subheading

YOU'LL GASP AT THE GEEK!

On the horizon in the distance, almost denying the reality of what we are seeing, tower vast cranes of unimaginable height while beyond them impossibly huge oil-drums squat against the moon-bright but cloudy sky.

Into shot, and running down the midway, comes a girl, TIFFANY.

TIFFANY is a girl in her early teens but looks younger then her years due to her boyish figure and her slightly over- delicate features.

For the last months, TIFFANY has been finding ways out of the institute and making her way here, where she has one special obsession, which we will soon see.

Following her into shot, but many yards behind, come two INTERNS from the Institute. They contrast each other almost comically, one being tall and plump while the other is smaller and thinner.

They're not quite the Stan and Ollie of the medical world but with some serious rehearsal they could get there.

1st INTERN

Oh, Jesus -she's gonna make it.

Even as the first INTERN says this, we see TIFFANY make a sharp left turn into a stall entrance.

EXT. HALL OF MIRRORS ENTRANCE NIGHT

A front view of the stall into which TIFFANY has run. The large sign above it proclaims 'HALL OF MIRRORS' and a smaller sign perched above a distorting mirror to one side of the entrance says 'YOU'LL BE AMAZED'.

The two INTERNS enter at a run.

INT. HALL OF MIRRORS NIGHT

There follows a hopelessly one-sided pursuit through the mirror maze as TIFFANY effortlessly eludes the two INTERNS.

There are three major facets to this sequence;

1) Comic relief - as the two interns make fools of themselves.

There could even be a room of distorting mirrors where the thin

INTERN becomes fat and the fat one thin.

2) TIFFANY'S ease and expertise with patterns and puzzles.

3) Confusion of the audience's sense of the real and the unreal.

This goes on long enough for us to realise the 1ST INTERN was right to worry, how long TIFFANY could elude them. Then, jarringly, as the screen is full of reflected TIFFANYS there suddenly appears amongst them a single image of

MALAHIDE.

Everything stops.
The image of MALAHIDE (and we shouldn't he sure yet if we're looking at a reflection or the real man) puts its hands out, palms up.

MALAHIDE
Tiffany. Come.
All the TIFFANYS move quietly toward him until they all disappear from view. Then the real TIFFANY comes into shot, her back to us, and walks toward what we now see to be the real MALAHIDE, who is standing in a doorway deliberately framed like a mirror to confuse the customers.
TIFFANY places her hands docilely on to MALAHIDE's outstretched ones.

INT. HOSPITAL ROOM NIGHT
KIRSTY has been dozing fitfully, but is awakened by strange noises. At first terrified, she slowly realises it is simply someone being put in the room next door.
She waits until activity has ceased and then moves to her door.
It is unlocked. She moves out into the corridor.

INT. HOSPITAL CORRIDOR NIGHT
Looking warily from side to side, KIRSTY edges out into the corridor, along it, and then stops by the door of the adjoining room.

INT. TIFFANY'S ROOM NIGHT C.U.
A hand fits a piece of jig-saw puzzle into the space it belongs.
We know it is a jig-saw by the shape of the pieces, but it is clearly not the conventional type - a picturesque photo - because all we can see at this close-up angle are large areas of black and white.

INT. TIFFANY'S ROOM NIGHT
We now see that the puzzle is on the floor of a room of a similar size to KIRSTY'S. It is slightly more decorated; It has curtains and wallpaper. And a tiled floor. Sitting cross-legged on the floor next to the puzzle is TIFFANY.
The puzzle, which we can now see more clearly, is an intricate abstract design in black and white. There are several pieces still un-fitted but TIFFANY is working steadily, efficiently, and with complete concentration.
On a wall behind her there is a visual record of her progress over the last few months. Sealed in plastic by staff members are.
Puzzles she has solved, with dates marking her advancement. They begin with the simplest wood block animals usually given to very small children. passing through photo-puzzles of increasing difficulty, and culminating in one or two other examples of the kind of complicated pattern-work she is involved in now.

INT. HOSPITAL CORRIDOR NIGHT
We pull out to see that this is KIRSTY'S P.O.V. from the glass panel in the door of TIFFANY'S room.

TIFFANY looks up at one point and eye-contact is made. KIRSTY gives a tentative smile and a small wave. TIFFANY stares at her.
The stare is long but unresponsive and finally TIFFANY returns to the puzzle.
KIRSTY has her back to us and the camera is quite close in when a hand suddenly moves into shot and touches her shoulder.
KIRSTY jumps back in alarm, fear on her face. But it is only

KYLE.
KYLE raises his hand in apology.

KYLE
Oh, Jesus, I'm sorry. God, if anyone should know not to do that, it's me. I'm sorry. O.K.?
KIRSTY nods and gives a nervous smile. KYLE, still embarrassed by his foolishness and eager to change the subject, nods towards the glass panel.

KYLE
Sad, huh? She's been here six months. Her name's TIFFANY.

KIRSTY
What's the matter with her?

KYLE
Almost complete withdrawal. She hasn't said a word for nearly two years.

KIRSTY
God, that's terrible.

KYLE
Yeah. Doctor Malahide's got her doing these jig-saws and things, though. Says it's helping to bring her out.
KYLE ushers KIRSTY back into her own room.

INT. HOSPITAL ROOM DAY
As he closes the door to KIRSTY's room, KYLE reaches into the pocket of his lab-coat and produces a small box of pills.

KYLE
Anyway, let's concentrate on you for a moment. Wanna suck on this for me?
KIRSTY looks up at him sharply. He is proffering a pill and grinning facetiously.

KIRSTY
Hey, good joke, Kyle. Do you always come on to the mentally ill?
KYLE's face falls. He blushes. Pressing the pills into KIRSTY's hand, he backs off to the door, apologising.

KYLE

Shit. Sorry. Here's the pills. Red face. Door. Bye.

He exits hurriedly, closing the door behind him. KIRSTY grins despite herself. She looks at the pill for a second or two and then puts it firmly back in the box. Realising there is no bedside table, she puts the box on the wooden chair.

KIRSTY
Jesus, I'm glad I'm not paying for this place.

She is about to lie down on the bed, when she senses something is wrong in the room.
KIRSTY is instantly tense again. She swings her head to the side and tenses in horror, stifling a scream.
In the corner of the room, against the wall lying in a pool of blood, is her skinned father LARRY.
KIRSTY emits a pained moan of pure anguish as she realises what she is looking at.

KIRSTY
(under her breath)
Daddy...

The thing in the corner raises its arm weakly from its side and begins to write on the wall in its own blood.
It writes : I AM IN HELL; HELP ME.
KIRSTY covers her eyes with her hands and begins to sob.
KIRSTY takes her hands from her eyes.
The figure has gone. The pool of blood has disappeared. But, on the wall the words remain.
KIRSTY makes herself rise from the bed and walk slowly across the room.
Her eyes full of tears, she stretches out her arm and touches the word 'I'.
As her fingers make contact, the words instantly disappear.
She presses her bloodied finger quickly to her lips before that last trace of her father can vanish, too.

INT. TIFFANY'S ROOM NIGHT
TIFFANY is still sitting up cross-legged, weeping. Her puzzle is completed.

EXT. THE INSTITUTE DAY
Basically an establishing shot to show it is the next morning but it also serves to show MALAHIDE walking briskly to work. His suit is tasteful and simple, but discreetly expensive-looking. He walks with purpose and looks straight ahead, acknowledging only with polite nods the respectful greetings of various JUNIOR
DOCTORS and NURSES he passes on his way. He enters the institute.
We should also see several patients being walked, or wheeled, around by STAFF during this shot.

MALAHIDE
(off-camera)
And how are we feeling today...?

INT. LARGE WARD DAY
This is a large, traditional hospital ward with a line of beds down each long wall and a wide central aisle.
Nearly all of the beds are occupied and, at the far end of the ward, there is a male patient in a wheelchair.
All the PATIENTS' eyes turn immediately and happily to MALAHIDE as he crosses the room, continuing his speech.

MALAHIDE
Better? Good.
He-doesn't stop his progress but walks straight through the room and into the corridor.
As the door closes behind him the WHEELCHAIR PATIENT scowls.

W/CHAIR PATIENT
105 years and he still doesn't know my name.

INT. HOSPITAL CORRIDOR DAY
MALAHIDE walks swiftly down the corridor in which we saw him talk to RONSON earlier, but this time the camera follows him through the double doors and further down the corridor.
He enters an elevator and the doors close in front of him.

INT. BASEMENT CORRIDOR DAY
MALAHIDE exits the elevator into a lower corridor, one not so carefully decorated.
We are in the area in which the more deeply disturbed of the
Institute's patients live.
The rooms are smaller, closer together, and there is an observation panel set in each door.
MALAHIDE looks into the first four rooms.
In the first, a middle-aged, overweight woman sits completely motionless in the middle of the floor. She is dressed in a shapeless white robe and is sitting crosslegged. Her head is shaven, her eyes are rolled completely up into the sockets so that only white shows.
In the second, a very thin man of about thirty is pressed as tight as he can be into one corner of the room. His hair is long and he has a full beard. He is naked but not unadorned - his body and much of his cell wall is smeared in excrement.
In the third, a man of about MALAHIDE'S age-stands in the centre of the room. He is of normal build but his head is shaved. His face, scalp, and hands are covered in self-inflicted and amaterurish tattoos- all of crosses. He is dressed in T-shirt and jeans. With both hands he holds aloft a silver crucifix, pointing it in all directions, as if under constant siege by Devils. He mutters prayers and invocations constantly.
In the fourth, a man in his early twenties restrained in a strait-jacket. He shuffles around on the call-floor, his eyes twitching and flitting from one part of his body to another.

BROWNING
(muttering)
Get them off me. Get them off me.

Off-camera, we hear the sound of KIRSTY's sobbing - which bridges the CUT TO:

INT. HOSPITAL ROOM DAY
KYLE enters, having heard KIRSTY crying. She is sitting with her legs over the side
of the bed with her face in her hands.
KYLE immediately sits next to her and puts an arm around her shoulder. He doesn't
force her to speak. He lets her let the tears out. Finally, she looks up.

KIRSTY
I...I had a visitor.

KYLE
What?

KIRSTY
Oh, Jesus. I can't explain. It's
...it's. I don't know how to help! I have to save him and I don't know how to help!

KYLE
(Carefully)
Kirsty, I'm sorry... don't understand. I...

KIRSTY
I know. No-one can. But I have to save him. Where's the other doctor? He said
He'd listen. He promised.
KYLE responds quickly to this. His faith in MALAHIDE is strong, despite that curious
incident of the previous night when
MALAHIDE followed RONSON out of the room.

KYLE
Dr. Malahide. Yes. Look, I'll fetch him. You take it easy.
I'm sure he can help.
KYLE stands up, making soothing motions with his hands, and heads for the door.

KIRSTY
Help. No, no-one can help. I just want someone to listen or I WILL go crazy.

KYLE
If anyone can help, HE can.
KIRSTY turns and gives KYLE a strange look as he opens the door.

KIRSTY
Yeah? He got a ticket to Hell?

INT. HOSPITAL CORRIDOR DAY

We TRACK with KYLE down the corridor, eventually reaching an impressive door, which is slightly ajar. Even before we reach it, we hear MALAHIDE's voice. He is clearly on the phone. Because of the nature of what he is hearing, KYLE pauses when he reaches the door, listening with a confused expression on his face.

MALAHIDE
(off-camera & gradually fading up)
Officer Kucich? Yes, Doctor
Malahide. You've spoken to
Ronson? Yes ... That's right.
The mattress ... No, I'll meet you by the side entrance. No, no, my HOUSE. Yes, let me make that clear. The house, NOT the hospital.
... Yes ... Fine, and thank you.
We hear the phone click. KYLE waits a moment and then walks swiftly through the door, speaking as he does so.

KYLE
Doctor Malahide ... ?

INT. HOSPITAL ROOM DAY
KIRSTY'S face fills the screen. Her voice is slightly dreamy, as if she is still trying to understand herself the story she is about to tell.

KIRSTY
It must have been going on forever...
Her voice trails off. We pull out to see KIRSTY sitting up on her bed. MALAHIDE on the wooden chair, and KYLE standing by the door.
MALAHIDE's voice pulls her back.

MALAHIDE
Kirsty...?
KIRSTY snaps back and continues to speak in a more normal voice.

KIRSTY
But the part I know about,
That must have started with my Uncle Frank...

MALAHIDE
Then let us speak of it ...

DISSOLVE TO
36 EXT. MALAHIDE's HOUSE TWILIGHT
We TRACK in slowly towards a modern house that we will learn is MALAHIDE'S, up the drive, towards the front door.

DISSOLVE TO

INT. MALAHIDE'S HALLWAY TWILIGHT
The TRACK continues along the hallway and into the OBSESSION

ROOM.
INT. OBSESSION ROOM NIGHT
The TRACK continues.
The room is dim, lit only by stray shafts of moonlight.
On the floor in the centre of the room is the mattress.
The TRACK stops. A main light is clicked on and MALAHIDE moves into shot.
MALAHIDE pours himself a scotch from the decanter that sits on the writing table and
approaches the mattress.
He is clearly very, excited. He walks around the mattress two or three times, never
taking his eyes off it.
He walks back to the writing table, throws his drink back, puts the glass down and leaves
the room.

EXT. MALAHIDE'S HOUSE NIGHT
MALAHIDE leaves through his front door and walks toward the hospital.

INT. OBSESSION ROOM NIGHT
After a few seconds silence we hear a repeated clicking sound, as if something is being
forced, followed by a louder snap and the sound of a sash window being opened.
The curtains balloon inwards, part, and KYLE steps into the room.
He stands still for a moment, as if making sure he is alone, and then begins to take in
his surroundings.
The room is entirely devoted to MALAHIDE'S secret obsession - with the Paranormal
in general and the Lament Configuration in particular.
It is a fair-sized, square shaped room. Prints, paintings, and photographs cover the walls.
All of these pictures relate in some way to his obsession; photographs of ghost-
sightings; portraits of magicians from Cagliostro to Crowley; prints of arcane symbols
and pentagrams, etc.
Specifically, we recognize a print that resembles very closely the jigsaw he has had
TIFFANY recently solve. Also, there are framed diagrams (which look very old) of the
Lament Configuration
-Both open and closed.
On a long, low table there are three glass cases. In each of these cases is a Lament
Configuration. On each case is a small label giving a location, a date of acquisition, and
a number - which we may assume to be the number of deaths attributable to that specific
box.
These labels read: CAIRO 3/4/'59 7

LYONS //'
NEW YORK //'
There are also, on a small desk-top bookshelf on a writing table, editions of
MALAHIDE'S own books. He seems to have spent his career publicly denying what he

is privately obsessed with - because the books titles include 'Possession: Not Demons but

Disease','The Myth of the Diabolic', and 'The Internal Inferno'.

KYLE
Jesus Christ. Jee-sus-kerr-ist!
We assume he has visited MALAHIDE'S house before, but he has clearly never seen this room.
He stares at the mattress with incredulity, as if he still can't believe his superior has had it brought here. Then he begins to look around the room in more detail. He approaches the glass cases and bends slightly to look at their contents.
KYLE shakes his head.

KYLE
Oh, shit.

INT. BASEMENT CORRIDOR NIGHT
MALAHIDE walks past a bank of meters and huge circuit breakers on his way to the lower and of the corridor, by the cells of the very disturbed. He stops by the cell of the man in the strait-jacket. We hear from the outside the familiar muttering of BROWNING. MALAHIDE enters the call.

INT. BROWNING'S CELL NIGHT
As MALAHIDE enters, BROWNING looks at him. His eyes demand, not plead, and he speaks through clenched teeth.

BROWNING
Get them off me. Get. Them.
Off. Me.

INT. OBSESSION ROOM NIGHT
KYLE is rooting through the drawers in the writing table.
Generally the contents are unremarkable - handwritten notes, a few patients case-files etc. - but in one of the drawers he finds a black ring-binder which he takes out and lays on the table.
It is a book of faces. There are about fifteen sheets in the binder. Some of them are genuine photographic prints, some photocopies of original photos. They range widely in age, race, and sex. They are all full-face portraits. Chronologically, the range is extensive too. Some pictures (generally photocopies) appear to date from the earliest days of photography, the late

1880's, others have an Edwardian appearance, or suggest the

1920's. Only one or two seem to be less than thirty years old.
KYLE flicks back and forward in the book, wondering on the significance of these people.
He is lost in the musings when the click of the front door tells him MALAHIDE has returned.

KYLE closes the book and quickly slips it back into the drawer.
He heads rapidly for the window he came in through but realises
MALAHIDE is too close for him to open it and make good his escape. Instead he stands between the window and the curtains, pulling the latter closed over him.
MALAHIDE enters the room, leading BROWNING who is still strait- jacketed.

INT. BEHIND THE CURTAIN NIGHT
We see KYLE standing very still in the limited space behind the curtains. It is clearly seen that, given the thoroughness with which he closed the curtains and his immobile position, he is unable to see what is happening in the room. He can hear, but not see.

INT. OBSESSION ROOM NIGHT
MALAHIDE leads BROWNING across to the mattress. Standing beside it, he unbuckles and removes the strait-jacket from his patient.
BROWNING, beneath the strait-jacket, is naked to the waist. His arms and cheat are a mass of scars of various age and size.
MALAHIDE gestures to the mattress. Now that his arms are free,
BROWNING is scratching furiously.

MALAHIDE
Mr. Browning. Please, lie down.
BROWNING lies down, still scratching, trust and hope in his eyes.

INT. OBSESSION ROOM BROWNING'S DELUSION (BROWNING'S P.O.V.)
As if looking through BROWNING's eyes, we see his body stretched out before us on the mattress.
The naked chest and arms are covered with raised lumps, red and painful-looking.
As his scratching arms attack these lumps, they break open, revealing vile black insects that have hatched beneath his skin.
BROWNING brushes these away while he scratches at the remaining lumps.

INT. OBSESSION ROOM NIGHT
BROWNING has already re-opened some of the more recent scars, and blood slowly rises to the surface of his skin.
MALAHIDE walks over to his writing tableland goes into one of the drawers.
He produces an old-fashioned cut-throat razor and walks back to

BROWNING
MALAHIDE
Here. This will help.
He proffers the razor. BROWNING siezes it. MALAHIDE steps back quickly, a mixture of anticipation and apprehension on his face.
BROWNING slashes at his body and left arm with a short, sharp, slicing motions. In his mind, he is lancing the cysts that contain the tormenting insects. In reality, he is inflicting horrifying damage on himself.

Blood pours from the multitude of wounds, running over his body and down onto the mattress.

Suddenly, without any preliminaries, two painfully thin, flayed, mucus-covered arms shoot out of the mattress, one on either side of the still-busy BROWNING.

They wrap themselves tightly across his chest and crush him tightly to the mattress, as a head, similarly wasted, oozes out of the mattress to the side of BROWNING's head.

Beneath his delusions, BROWNING suddenly has an inkling of what is happening to him. His eyes widen and his mouth opens ready to emit a scream but the monster beneath him forces a hand over his mouth as it buries its face into the soft flesh of his neck.

Two legs now rise from the oozing slime that the bloodstains on the mattress have become. They too wrap themselves around

BROWNING so that he is held tight.

Finally, with titanic effort, he gathers enough momentum to roll completely free of the mattress and falls to the floor beside it.

The thing on his back now is pulling free from the bed of bubbling, frothing slime that the mattress now is with a sliding, slurping sound.

The monster's face is now deep in the flesh of his throat, and even as BROWNING forces himself up first onto one knee and then, very unsteadily, onto his feet, we can see him wasting away - his face losing its fullness and colour, his chest sinking in on itself. The creature, which is still wrapped around him and clinging tight is, unlike him, growing in stature by the second. Muscles are inflating, arteries pumping more vigorously, and flesh itself filling out.

Its horrific thin-ness when it first appeared effectively unsexed it but now, as its regeneration continues, the fullness of its hips, the roundness of its thighs, and the sacs of fat and muscle that bloom above its ribs confirm its female nature. If there was any doubt that this was JULIA, it is now disappearing.

BROWNING is now nearly a walking corpse and it is the strength of his will alone that allows him to take a few faltering steps with

JULIA still enveloping him. With the desperate strength with which she clings to him and the way her legs are wrapped around his hips, it is like an obscenely perverse parody of sexual passion.

MALAHIDE has been watching all this with an incredible mix of emotions playing across his face. Still human enough to feel both fear and disgust at what is happening he is nevertheless awe struck and exhilarated. He has waited all his life for such an irrefutable demonstration of the power and the truth of the supernatural.

Similarly, the scientist in him is fascinated by the living anatomy lessons that JULIA's regeneration and BROWNING rapid decay offer.

With one last dying effort, the now-almost-husk-like BROWNING breaks JULIA'S grip and makes a futile step forward as she falls from him. He totters towards the curtains.

Just as the audience think he will pull them down with him, revealing KYLE, JULIA grabs his ankle and pulls. He falls back to the floor.

INT. BEHIND THE CURTAINS NIGHT

The loud noise of BROWNING's fall renews KYLE's resolve to see what is going on. Carefully, he shifts his position so that he can see through a small gap in the curtains.

INT. KYLE'S P.O.V. NIGHT
KYLE may have heard one or two strange and unpleasant noises but
BROWNING has not screamed nor JULIA spoken; nothing has prepared him for what
he sees - a skinned woman sucking out what life remains from the dried husk of a
psychotic man.

INT. BEHIND THE CURTAINS NIGHT
KYLE's head jerks back, shaking as if he's just had an electric shock. His mouth moves
but no sound emerges.

KYLE
(mimed)
Jesus Christ!
His terror simultaneously urging speed and silence, KYLE gingerly maneuvers himself
out of the window.

INT. OBSESSION ROOM NIGHT
JULIA lies back satisfied on the floor. She looks up weakly at

MALAHIDE.
JULIA
Help me.
Her voice is perfect. MALAHIDE stares at her, his fascination intense. He crosses the
few yards that separate them. He looks at her, lying beside the hollow shell that was
CHEYNEY. Her eyes stare back, brilliant, sparkling, alive.

JULIA
Help Me.
MALAHIDE realises her temporary vulnerability; all the life force she has absorbed
from BROWNING has made up her body, but it will take some moments for the
strength to return to her.
Fascinated and sympathetic as he is however he cannot yet quite brine himself to touch
this creature. Instead he moves the mattress nearer to her, allowing her to crawl back
onto it and lie down again.
MALAHIDE stares down at her. He attempts a smile, but is too nervous to make it
convincing. He is trembling slightly. This contact with the beyond is something he has
dreamt of for years, but nevertheless the physical reality is overwhelming.
JULIA treats him to the approximation of a smile. She is far from nervous.
She studies herself. Her figure is fully formed, her womanliness undeniable. All she is
missing is a skin. She stretches her arms.
She lifts her legs. She writhes on the bed in pleasure, like an X- ray photograph of a
calendar girl.
MALAHIDE stares at her, following the sensual movements of her body. He swallows,
a little embarrassed by his response to the naked display he is privileged to watch.
JULIA'S eyes twinkle at him.

JULIA

Don't be embarrassed. You're my friend.

She looks away and continues her stretching and wiggling, more conscious of it now as an erotic display.

The strength has flooded through her body as she rises to her feet, and stops off the mattress, smiling at MALAHIDE.

MALAHIDE backs away from her as she moves towards him, doing his best to return her smile.

After a few steps, JULIA stops and simply stares into MALAHIDE'S eyes. He too stops and returns the gaze. The camera circles them slowly several times, studying them - the dressed, nervous man and skinned, confident woman.

JULIA

Well?

MALAHIDE says nothing. Perhaps he swallows nervously. The camera continues its circling movements. The scene FADES TO BLACK and

JULIA begins to laugh, small, sensual giggles at first building finally as the blackness comes into an almost hysterical crescendo of raucous joy.

INT. HOSPITAL ROOM NIGHT

KIRSTY is again lying on her back on top of the bed. She is a stark contrast to JULIA. No display. No laughter.

Her eyes are open and red-rimmed from weeping now. There is also complete silence.

All the more jarring, then, the sudden sound of someone fumbling at the handle of KIRSTY'S door.

Her eyes widen in alarm and she flings herself off the bed, scanning the room for anything that can be used as a weapon.

There is nothing but the chair and she she has all but lifted it aloft when she sees that it is KYLE, who comes into the room.

KIRSTY

Shit, Kyle. This is getting to be a habit. What is it, some kind of shock-therapy?

She was angry, relieved, and amused when she realized it was KYLE and all these showed in her voice and face. Now they drop away completely, replaced by a nervous apprehension as she becomes aware of the blank horror on his face.

KIRSTY

Oh, Jesus. What is it?

KYLE opens his mouth a few times, as if unsure what to say.

KYLE

It's all true.

INT. TIFFANY'S ROOM NIGHT

TIFFANY walks around her room, staring at her completed puzzles - those on the wall and the one on the floor - and waiting for the next one.

FADE OUT
FADE IN
EXT. MALAHIDE'S HOUSE DAY
A simple shot tells us it is the next morning.

INT. OBSESSION ROOM MALAHIDE'S HOUSE DAY
MALAHIDE , dressed in a black suit, is in the room, staring at the empty mattress. We TRACK with him through to his LIVING ROOM.

INT. LIVING ROOM MALAHIDE'S HOUSE DAY
In contrast to the secret and private obsession room, this room is the tasteful and upmarket room of the successful professional.
It is a long spacious room with modern furniture and white walls.
The walls are mostly free of decoration save for two or three large canvases of abstract art.
The longest wall is broken up only by a low circular table, which rests against it about half way down. On this table is a very simple black vase containing a spray of beautiful white lilies.
Above this vase on the wall is a large frameless mirror.
As MALAHIDE enters, the first thing he sees is a bloody palm- print on one of his white walls. He blinks at it and looks down into the room. We CUT TO;
JULIA. At first it seems she is staring at the lilies, but as we
TRACK around her, we realise she is staring at the reflection of her skinned self.
Her face snarls at herself, she roars with rage, forms her hand into a fist and shatters the mirror.
MALAHIDE rushes towards her. She swings round and freezes him with a glance.
They hold their positions for a moment, MALAHIDE nervous and
JULIA furious, and then JULIA makes herself relax. She sighs, takes a few deep breaths, and then speaks.

JULIA
I'm cold.

TIME CUT
INT. LIVING ROOM MALAHIDE'S HOUSE DAY
CLOSE UP on a strangely Art Deco electric fan heater, with bright red coils emitting waves of heat.
We pull out to see MALAHIDE standing by the table with the flowers.
There is now a half-full glass of wine on the table, along with an ashtray where a cigarette burns away ignored. A pack of cigarettes is now visible in the breast pocket of MALAHIDE's jacket.

JULIA enters the room and closes the door behind her. She is dressed in one of MALAHIDE'S suits. It is a light weight suit of white linen, a suit for expensive holidays in hot countries.

She crosses the room to the table; pausing slightly in the centre of the room, to allow MALAHIDE to look at her.

JULIA
Well?
MALAHIDE'S nervousness has retreated a little, he manages to smile. He nods his head slowly a few times.

MALAHIDE
Yes... Yes. You look...

JULIA
Surreal? Strange? Nightmarish?

MALAHIDE
No. You look...
He pauses, lost for words.
JULIA doesn't wait for an answer. She crosses to the table and takes up his glass of wine. She downs it in one.
MALAHIDE stares at her, a little surprised.

JULIA
Yes, I still like WINE ...
She smiles strangely at him and then moves closer. Slowly, keeping her eyes on his, she reaches into his breast pocket for his packet of cigarettes and places one in her mouth.

JULIA
... and more.
For a moment, MALAHIDE's face is stone. Then, slowly, he returns her smile and, drawing his lighter, lights her cigarette.

INT. SHOPPING MALL DAY
A large multi-level shopping complex obviously up-market and expensive.
We see MALAHIDE, riding up one on the central escalators, looking around him as he does so, as if searching for a specific shop.
He reaches the next level and begins to walk along one of the several avenues that lead away from the central square containing the escalators.
He walks past several shops, looking in their windows; a chic specialty shop, a window full of clocks, a cutler's. Finally, he stops in front of one. He stares at its display window. The window is classily minimal. There is in fact only one dress in it. It is an exquisite white cocktail gown. The gown is full length but quite tight-fitting, merely flaring a little from below the knee, and has a halter-neck.
MALAHIDE walks into the shop.

INT. MALAHIDE'S BEDROOM DAY
We are looking at a reflection of MALAHIDE in the large mirror that covers the inside of his wardrobe door. His real hand and his reflected hand come together at the edge of the door and tip it slightly, changing the image that the mirror shows us.
Now we see JULIA. She is in the dress from the shop in the mall.
It is a perfect fit and shows her figure off very well. Being a halter-neck, however, her skinned arms and shoulders are completely bare. Also, it is quite low cut at the front, exposing a fair degree of visceral cleavage, and at the back.
JULIA turns fully around in front of the mirror examining herself from every angle. Her mood is unreadable until she speaks.

JULIA
Close it.
MALAHIDE does so. He understands and tries to console her..

MALAHIDE
It's a beautiful dress...

JULIA
I know.

TIME CUT
INT. LIVING ROOM MALAHIDE'S HOUSE DAY
CLOSE UP MALAHIDE'S hands applying wide, white, surgical bandages to JULIA. We pull out as MALAHIDE steps away from JULIA. They are both standing in the middle of the living room floor.
JULIA'S arms, torso, and head are now completely enclosed in neatly and professionally applied bandages. There are three slits for her eyes and mouth but apart from these she is completely covered. Over these she is still wearing the white dress.

MALAHIDE
There...
JULIA lifts her arms slightly to look at them and then touches her bandaged face. She turns towards MALAHIDE. The camera begins the same circling movement it made around them the previous night.
MALAHIDE'S nervousness has practically disappeared. He has helped this woman. He has bandaged her and dressed her. He is slightly in awe of her, but it is now tinged with excitement, not fear.
The camera's circling grows faster.

MALAHIDE
Well?
JULIA walks towards him, slowly raising her hands. When she is close enough her hands cup his cheeks. She pulls him towards her, and, tipping her head to one side, kisses him. Her body moulds itself to his.

She leans her head back. Were they have kissed blood has pressed up onto the bandage from her skinned flesh. It looks like smeared lipstick.

JULIA
Well?
MALAHIDE puts his arms around her waist. They kiss tenderly.
Slowly, almost nervously, he lowers his hands until they rest on her buttocks and presses her in towards him. They begin to spin themselves now, echoing the camera movements.
They cross the room, kissing blindly, until they come to rest against the wall that bears JULIA's bloody palm print. JULIA twists their bodies so that MALAHIDE is pressed against the wall, and begins to move her hips forcefully and sensually against

MALAHIDE.
The camera is stationary now, watching without movement as
MALAHIDE begins to raise JULIA's dress up her legs, her hand on his wrist, helping and encouraging.
About halfway up the thigh, the bandaging disappears and the raw flesh is exposed.
The kissing and the fumbling continue until they are making fast and violent love against the wall.
His hands clutch tightly at her hips and he pulls his face away from the kissing to loan it on her shoulder so that we see his face as it grimaces in ecstasy.
He cries out and shudders and slowly both their movements stop.
He strokes at her back gently and their bodies relax.

JULIA
(almost coyly)
Now all we need is a skin.

INT. BATHROOM KYLE'S APARTMENT DAY
CLOSE UP on shower jets hitting KIRSTY's face and naked shoulders.
Her eyes are closed, but she smiles in pleasure as the water refreshes her.
A knocking is heard. KIRSTY moves her head out of the water's path and shouts.

KIRSTY
Yeah?

INT. KYLE'S APARTMENT DAY
It is basically a studio apartment - everything except the bathroom facilities is in the one room. There is a sofa - with sheets and blankets on it - a bed, a dining/all-purpose table with two chairs, shelves full of records and books, and a small working desk against one of the walls. The desk is weighed down by text books and notes and, tacked to the wall above it, are medical prints, some of the brain and central nervous system, but also two fullcoloured anatomical prints - one of a man and one of a woman. They could almost be portraits of JULIA and FRANK.

KYLE, fully dressed, is standing by the bathroom door, his hand still in a knocking position.

KYLE
You O.K.?
Silence.

KYLE
Kirsty? You 0. K.?
The bathroom door opens and KIRSTY Comes into the main room, dressed in a toweling robe that is clearly a 'hers' not a 'his'.
She crosses the room to a mirror, rubbing at her wet hair with a towel.

KIRSTY
No bad dreams.

KYLE
So you slept O.K.?
KIRSTY gestures at the sofa.

KIRSTY
As much as that bed of nails allowed.
KYLE glances meaningfully at the bed as he replies.

KYLE
Well, the sofa isn't often used for sleeping on...

KIRSTY
Oh yeah? On your own a lot,
Huh?
KYLE grins.

KYLE
Like the robe?
KIRSTY returns the smile via the mirror.
KYLE crosses the room to sit at his dining table. Empty coffee cups, the remnants of a loaf and some cheese suggests their breakfast was simple and finished some time ago.
KIRSTY gathers her clothes from by the sofa and moves back into the bathroom to dress.
KYLE waits a few moments and then speaks.

KYLE
I think I need to talk. About what I saw.
KIRSTY emerges, fully dressed, her hair still damp.

KIRSTY

You thought I was crazy, didn't you?
KYLE spreads his hands wide.

KYLE
Jesus, yes! What do you expect.
I mean, God, I still do! It's just that now I'm crazy too.
He grins wryly. KIRSTY moves to the sofa and sits down.

KIRSTY
And you're sure it was a woman?

KYLE
God, I wish I could say no.
This is going to do terrible things to my attitude, you know.
KIRSTY grins at him.

KIRSTY
Don't worry about it. Your attitude sucks anyway.

KYLE
Hey, so for it. Don't let pity stop you. I'm down. Nail me.
For a moment, they laugh together but then stop. KIRSTY stares downward and then
suddenly bursts into tears.

KIRSTY
What can I do? How can I save him?
KYLE joins her on the sofa. He offers an arm but she shakes it off.

KIRSTY
The box. I need the box.

KYLE
The box? Like in your story?
Like in his house?
KIRSTY's tears suddenly stop. She looks at KYLE.

KIRSTY
(sharply)
What?

KYLE
The Boxes. In the House. I told you.

KIRSTY
What do you mean?

KYLE
The boxes! I TOLD you.

KIRSTY
You DIDN'T tell me. Do you mean Malahide's got...

KYLE
Yeah. The things you were talking about.
KIRSTY heads instantly for KYLE'S door.

KIRSTY
I'm going.
KYLE runs across the room and puts a restraining hand on his door.

KYLE
Wait a minute. What do you mean,
'I'm going?' TO the HOUSE?
KIRSTY nods and pulls at the door handle.

KIRSTY
Get out of the way.

KYLE
Are you crazy?

KIRSTY
I don't know, Kyle. You're the fucking expert. Now get out of the way!

KYLE
WHY?
KIRSTY
(shouting)
Because I'm going to get my father!
Tears start to her eyes and she stares at KYLE defiantly. Then she repeats, more softly;

KIRSTY
I'm going to get my father.
There is a two-second silence between them as they stare at each other.
Finally, Kyle backs away from the door, raising a finger.

KYLE
Two seconds. Just two seconds.
Don't move.
He rushes across the room, grabs a jacket, and moves back to the door.

KYLE

O.K. Let's go.

KIRSTY
Kyle, you don't have...

KYLE
I KNOW I don't have to. It's just my time of the month to be a complete fucking idiot. O.K.?
KIRSTY stares at him, her face at first blank then suffused with emotion. She leans across and plants a chaste kiss on his lips then pulls back. There is a beat while they simply stare at each other and suddenly they are tight in each other's arms, kissing fervently. But the kiss is fuelled, not by passion, but by fear and their mutual need for human solace in the face of the unknown.
As the kiss continues, the camera pulls back from them.

INT. THE BLOOD-BOUDOIR DAY
CLOSE UP as JULIA (still bandaged) and MALAHIDE come together for a kiss. They part and, as JULIA moves across the room, the camera begins a long TRACK around the room.
First, it reaches a naked GIRL. As catatonic as TIFFANY, she says nothing but her eyes betray her terror. Her hands are tied above her.
JULIA moves in towards the girl, her eyes glittering with an alien hunger beneath their gauze mask. As she nears the girl, the TRACK passes them and moves through the room.
MALAHIDE has done his mistress proud. It had been an empty upstairs room (no furniture, bare floorboards) but now it resembles a nightmarish cross between a butcher's shop and a bordello.
The camera slowly reveals, as it TRACKS, that there are seven more people in the room. Seven dead people. Dried-out husks.
The TRACKING is now completing its circle around the room. After the corpses, we return to JULIA and the GIRL - but the GIRL too is now a hollow, dried-out shell.
JULIA moves back into the centre of the room and stands still.
MALAHIDE crosses the room to her quickly, drawing a wicked- looking kitchen knife from his pocket as he does so. He reaches
JULIA and raises the knife to her face.
With one swift, precise movement, he slices the bandages across the side of her face. JULIA raises her hand and pulls the mask away.
The camera sweeps in toward her as she does this until her face is in CLOSE UP as the bandage-mask is pulled aside.
Her face is perfect.

EXT. MALAHIDE'S HOUSE DAY
MALAHIDE emerges from his front door. He is still in his black suit and looks every inch the respectable professional. He looks neither left nor right but moves straight off, a busy man with things to do.

A few seconds after he has gone off-camera, KYLE and KIRSTY emerge from around the corner of the house.
KYLE gestures to KIRSTY to follow him and leads her around to the window he broke in through on the previous night.

INT. OBSESSION ROOM DAY
The room is much as we saw it last.
The window slides up and KYLE pulls himself into the room. He looks around it carefully. Sure that the monster he saw the previous night is no longer in the room, he helps KIRSTY in through the window.
KIRSTY's eyes go at once to the three LAMENT CONFIGURATIONS in the glass cases. She crosses the room eagerly.
KYLE rushes after her and stops her opening one of the cases.

KYLE
Wait! The .. thing ...
I want to be sure it's not here.
KIRSTY nods and KYLE leaves the room.

INT. STAIRS/LANDING MALAHIDE'S HOUSE DAY
KYLE advances carefully, and slowly, from the stairs onto the landing. He looks about him at every step he takes.
Ahead of him on the landing is a door, which is very slightly ajar.
He advances gingerly down the landing to the door.
When he reaches it, he pauses. We see his face working as he ponders his choices - should he push it open inch by slow inch, or slam it inwards quickly?
Very slowly he moves his hand towards the door. The camera matches his movement, moving in on his hand, the door, and the space between.
His fingertips are less than an inch from touching the door when another hand shoots into view and grabs his wrist.
JULIA has crept up beside him on the landing while all his attention was on the door.
KYLE swings round in horror, his mouth opening to scream when he sees that JULIA has her other hand to her mouth, her finger at her lips in a silencing gesture.
There is of course, nothing for him to recognize from the monstrous vision of the previous night. JULIA's arms, chest, and face are completely re-skinned now. All KYLE sees is a beautiful stranger in a white dress.

JULIA
Sssh. I think it's still here.

KYLE
What? The...The thing?
JULIA nods.

JULIA

Yes. I had to stop you going in there because I knew you'd cry out. Any normal person would.
It ...It's just TERRIBLE.

KYLE
Is it in there?

JULIA
No. Not now.
KYLE swallows, nods, and gently, pushes the door open. He walks into the room.

INT. THE BLOOD-BOUDOIR DAY
The camera follows KYLE into the room. He reaches the middle before horror and disgust stop him.
He hears a click behind him and turns to see JULIA has come into the room and closes the door behind her. She looks at KYLE.

JULIA
Was I right? Is it terrible?
KYLE stares all around him. All eight victims have been sucked dry. He is surrounded by dead husks.
His face is ghastly. He looks like he is about to faint. He nods.
His voice is a cracked whisper.

KYLE
Yes. Yes, it's terrible.
JULIA crosses the room rapidly towards him. Her face is a picture of concern.

JULIA
Oh. You look awful. You poor boy. Come here...
As she speaks, JULIA's arms are opening out to him. KYLE sees the comfort offered and advances towards her, too.
As they come together, the camera moves around them and we see, for the first time, that JULIA is still incomplete; Her entire back is still glistening raw flesh, the naked bones of the spine still clearly visible.
Their arms go around each other just as JULIA completes her speech;

JULIA
...Come to Mother ...
As KYLE's hands touch the sticky, mucoid meat of her shoulders, it is instantly clear to him what has happened. For a moment he freezes in terror.
His arms fly from her and he throws his head back. But JULIA is very strong now and her grip does not relax.
Kyle's expression is a mixture of terror and confusion as he stares into the beautiful face of the monster.
JULIA smiles at him, a hungry, aroused smile.

JULIA
What's your name?
KYLE can hardly speak for fear.

KYLE
Kyle...

JULIA
I'm JULIA.
She raised one hand from his back to the back of his head and presses his face to hers.
JULIA plays it exactly as a sensual, passionate kiss, her mouth wide open, her head moving rhythmically and sinuously.
KYLE's reaction is somewhat different; his arms flail in panic
(though only from the elbow - JULIA'S grip prevents anything more) and his head makes jerking, backward movements against her pressing hand.
The camera moves around the embracing couple until it is behind

JULIA.
The back of her gown, as we know, is extremely low. As the kiss continues, we see skin creeping above the line of the gown at the base of her spine and gradually flowing up her back until finally it meets and blends perfectly with ragged and raw edges of the skin at her neck and shoulders. JULIA is complete again.
While this process has been going on, KYLE has been dying slowly and horribly in her arms, his lifeforce being sucked into her through their open mouths. His body, by the time her back is completely formed, is shrunken, hollow, and dried up.
JULIA takes her arms from around the corpse of KYLE and steps back, allowing the husk to fall to the floor.
JULIA licks her lips and looks down, not without affection, at the dead KYLE. She smiles.

JULIA
Thank you, Kyle.

INT. OBSESSION ROOM DAY
KIRSTY has found the black ring-binder and laid it on the writing table.
She has separated one of the photographs from the others and laid it out on the table beside the binder. It is the ENGLISH OFFICER from the opening sequence. KIRSTY has obviously recognized something familiar in it but she can't quite grasp it completely. She is still puzzling over it when she suddenly realises that several minutes have elapsed since KYLE left her there. Her head straightens up and her puzzled look is replaced by a slightly worried one.

KIRSTY
(to herself)
Kyle...?

She folds up the photograph and puts it in her pocket.
She crosses to the door and opens it. She does not go through it immediately but stands in the doorway for a moment, her hand still on the door, cocking her head slightly as if listening.

KIRSTY
(slightly louder)
Kyle?
She can't hear anything, but she regards that as a bad sign, not a good one. She leaves the room.

INT. STAIRS/LANDING DAY
KIRSTY makes her way up the stairs. Unlike KYLE a little earlier she moves up them quite quickly and advances onto the landing.
When she is on the landing and looking at the closed door to
JULIA's Boudoir she stops, standing still and staring at the door.
KIRSTY suppresses a shudder. She bites her lip, takes two or three deep breaths, crosses to the door firmly, and flings it open, moving into the room even as she does so.

INT. THE BLOOD-BOUDOIR DAY
KIRSTY moves three or four steps into the room and then stops dead. The door swings shut behind her.
KIRSTY's eyes flick left and right, taking in the sickening details of the room's contents, and then stare straight ahead, focusing on the figure in white which is turning around to face her.
JULIA completes her turn and looks at KIRSTY completely impassively for a moment. Then her mouth opens up into a smile of welcome - but there is nothing but hate in her eyes.

JULIA
Kirsty! How nice of you to drop in.
JULIA glances meaningfully at the dead thing that lies beside her feet and then back at KIRSTY.

JULIA
You have surprisingly good taste in men.
KIRSTY's fear and disgust are momentarily displaced by a furious rage as she realises what JULIA has done. Her face erupts into anger and she screams out.

KIRSTY
Kyle! No! I'll kill you, you...
She flings herself across the room at JULIA even as she speaks.
JULIA is completely unphased by this attack and simply raises one arm. She siezes the wrist of the arm that KIRSTY has raised into a clenched fist and effortlessly throws KIRSTY bodily back across the room. We realise for the first time the immense physical strength that JULIA now possesses.

KIRSTY smashes into the door and falls to a sitting position against it. She is shaken and slightly hurt enough not to get to her feet immediately but she stares at JULIA with undimmed hatred.
JULIA throws a look halfway between a smile and a sneer.

JULIA
Oh, you can try it, you little bitch. I'd love you to try it. But I'm not just the woman I was.

KIRSTY
What, you mean you're something more than a whore with a vicious streak?

JULIA
I mean I'm something more than human, you little shit!
JULIA snaps this first line but then holds her anger in check.
She shakes her head and an amused smile plays across her lips.

JULIA
Oh, Kirsty. They didn't tell you, did they? I'm afraid they've changed the rules of the fairy tale; I'm no longer just the wicked step-mother.
The smile disappears and she delivers the next line with an utterly straight face. It is, after all, the truth.

JULIA
Now I'm the Evil Queen.
The hatred and the heat returns to her voice.

JULIA
So come on; Take your best shot, Snow White.
KIRSTY scrambles to her feet and again charges at JULIA.
JULIA steps forward to meet her advance and delivers a single back-handed swipe across KIRSTY's face with such force that not only is the girl knocked off her feet but is actually knocked unconscious.
KIRSTY rolls onto her back and lies at JULIA's feet.
JULIA stares down at the unconscious body. When it was awake, it was KIRSTY and her attitude to it was based on personal enmity.
Now, it is simply another body and she judges it differently; it is firm, full, healthy, and young. We see the expression on her face change from hatred and triumph to pure appetite. She licks her lips and her eyes glisten. She begins to bend slightly towards it.

MALAHIDE
(off-camera)
Julia!
The door to the room opens. JULIA straightens up and looks as
MALAHIDE stands in the doorway. Her eyebrows question this interruption.
A second later, and it is explained. He leads TIFFANY into the room.

TIME CUT
INT. OBSESSION ROOM DAY
TIFFANY sits cross-legged in the middle of the floor. She appears to be alone in the room. Cradled in her lap is a Lament
Configuration, taken from one of the glass cases on the low table.
On a wall behind TIFFANY, one of the large prints that previously hung there has been taken down.
Revealed in the space behind it is a large mirror. The camera moves in towards this mirror.

INT. OBSESSION ROOM ALCOVE DAY
MALAHIDE and JULIA stand in a tiny and completely bare room. On the wall in front of them is a large window through which we see a back-view of TIFFANY in the obsession room.

INT. OBSESSION ROOM DAY
TIFFANY looks around the room generally and then turns her attention completely to the LAMENT CONFIGURATION.
She picks it up and turns it around in her hands, studying each of its faces intently.
She begins trying to move the interlinked pieces within it. At first she has no success; the box appears to be one solid construction with no internal movement possible.
She stops her attempts and studies it again for a moment, her face still impassive. Then she gives a tiny smile and begins again.
Her movements are faster now, less tentative.
Suddenly, there is a click and one of the panels on-the box slides out slightly. The little music-box tune begins to play.
To TIFFANY this is a marvelous reward - something the jigsaw never offered - and she lets out a little sound in response, somewhere between a sigh and a delighted giggle. It tempts her to even greater skill and her delighted fingers fly over the box.
Another panel moves. Then two more. The tune is prettier and fuller.

INT. OBSESSION ROOM ALCOVE DAY
MALAHIDE stares fixedly through the window, nervous but terribly excited. He is breathing rapidly and shallowly.
Through the glass, TIFFANY's success continues. Small flashes of intense blue light begin to buzz around the box. The room grows darker and cracks begin to appear in its walls.
JULIA seems quietly amused - both by what is going on in the room and by MALAHIDE's heated response to it. She glances from one to the other, her eyes twinkling.

JULIA
You're sure this is what you want?
MALAHIDE doesn't take his eyes from the window.

MALAHIDE
It's what I've ALWAYS wanted. A view of ... beyond.
He pauses. Perhaps he is being ungallant. He turns slightly towards JULIA and takes
her hand.

MALAHIDE
You were almost enough, Julia but...I have to see. I have to

KNOW.
JULIA smiles indulgently. She nods.

JULIA
Oh, I quite understand.

INT. OBSESSION ROOM DAY
TIFFANY is completely engrossed in the box. She seems blissfully unaware of the
changes taking place in the room.
The cracks have widened in the walls and, in some places, pieces of plaster have fallen
away, revealing the slats beneath.
Blue light begins to stream into the room, ignoring the geography of what should lie
beyond its walls. Where the light comes through the slats, it is as broad beams of light,
given contrast by the shadows of the slats. But it also comes through the smaller cracks
and enters the room in intensely bright and very thin beams that criss-cross through the
room almost like a laser display.
Suddenly, TIFFANY's solution is complete. The central core of the box rises up and
twists itself around into its final position.

INT. OBSESSION ROOM ALCOVE DAY
MALAHIDE takes an almost involuntary step backward. His excitement has now
reached the pitch where it is beyond obvious physical manifestation. He is perfectly
still, his face perfectly impassive.

MALAHIDE
She's done it.

JULIA
She certainly has.

MALAHIDE
It's coming.

JULIA
It certainly is.
MALAHIDE turns away to meet her eyes.
There is a beat or two where absolutely nothing happens.
The mirror explodes inwards into the alcove.

INT. OBSESSION ROOM DAY
The room is filled with smoke and suffused with blue light.
Two of the walls simply part physically, revealing entrances into the corridors of Hell.
These corridors are lined with gray walls and seem to run for a great distance.
TIFFANY still sits cross-legged in the middle of the floor, staring about her in astonishment.
Surrounding her, in various parts of the room, are the four
CENOBITES from HELLRAISER.
The FEMALE CENOBITE smiles and advances towards TIFFANY.
The leader of the CENOBITES, PINHEAD raises a hand.

PINHEAD
Wait.
The FEMALE stops and looks questioningly at PINHEAD.
PINHEAD, at a more leisurely pace, crosses towards TIFFANY and looks down at her.
She stares back at him, the remnants of her insanity a temporary defense against fear, her face registering nothing.
PINHEAD looks up.

PINHEAD
No.
The FEMALE looks across at him.

CENOBITE
No?
PINHEAD shakes his head.

PINHEAD
No.
He glances down at TIFFANY again.

PINHEAD
It is not HANDS that call us...
He looks up and stares directly at the shattered two-way mirror.

PINHEAD
... It is DESIRE.

INT. OBSESSION ROOM ALCOVE DAY
The wall opposite the shattered mirror has also opened up to reveal a way into Hell.
MALAHIDE and JULIA are no longer in the alcove.
We hear the ringing of their footsteps. They are making their way down the corridor.

INT. OBSESSION ROOM DAY
The four CENOBITES have gone.

TIFFANY looks around the room again. She stares from one entrance to the other. Her manner is reminiscent of when she is making decisions during her solving of puzzles.

INT. BLOOD-BOUDOIR DAY
KIRSTY is still on the floor in the boudoir of blood. This room too is now suffused with blue light and smoke. There are no gateways to Hell in the walls but there are several cracks in the plaster and these appear to be spreading.
KIRSTY moans and opens her eyes gingerly. She puts a hand to her face, rubbing at the place where JULIA hit her.
Still a little groggy, she lifts herself slowly to a sitting position, her legs stretched out. Only when she has blinked a few times, shaken her head, and rubbed her jaw again, does full consciousness return - at which point she looks quickly about the room (possibly expecting another attack from JULIA) and notices the light and the smoke.
She has been in this atmosphere before. She knows precisely what it means. Her mouth opens and her eyes grow nervous again.

KIRSTY
Oh, shit.
KIRSTY scrambles quickly to her feet and rushes through the door to the stairs.

INT. OBSESSION ROOM DAY
KIRSTY enters the room just as TIFFANY is about to go down one of the corridors. KIRSTY screams at her.

KIRSTY
NO!
TIFFANY stops, startled, and looks at the doorway and KIRSTY.
KIRSTY raises her hands in a placatory gesture and speaks more softly.

KIRSTY
Wait. Wait.
KIRSTY begins to move into the room slowly and shakes her head gently.

KIRSTY
Hey, remember me? From the hospital? I was in the next room?
KIRSTY is rewarded with a small recognizing smile from TIFFANY,
KIRSTY returns the smile.

KIRSTY
You don't want to go down there. You REALLY don't want to go down there.
TIFFANY turns her head once more to look down the corridor and then turns back to KIRSTY. For a second it looks as if KIRSTY's persuasions have succeeded, but MALAHIDE's training has been too thorough; TIFFANY knows a puzzle when she sees one. She smiles once more at KIRSTY and then suddenly turns and disappears into the corridor.

KIRSTY stands still for a moment, as if she can't quite believe that TIFFANY has done it. She shakes her head - half in disbelief and half in despair.

KIRSTY
Jesus Christ.
Pausing only to pick up the LAMENT CONFIGURATION from where
TIFFANY has left it on the floor, She heads straight for the corridor and follows
TIFFANY in.

INT. CORRIDORS/LABYRINTH
We are looking straight down one of the very long corridors of
Hell.
It has the same architecture as the corridor that appeared in the hospital room in
HELLRAISER; walls of stained gray stone broken up by vaguely medieval-looking
arches.
KIRSTY comes into view, walking away from the camera. Ahead of her, at an
illogically far distance given that she entered the corridor only seconds before KIRSTY,
is TIFFANY.
KIRSTY breaks into a slight run, and calls out to the girl.

KIRSTY
Tiffany. Wait!
Her voice has an unpleasant ring in the acoustics of these corridors and echos horribly.
KIRSTY pulls a face and doesn't shout again. She increases her pace slightly.
Suddenly TIFFANY makes a sharp turn and enters an intersecting corridor. KIRSTY is
forced to increase her speed even more.
KIRSTY too makes the turn into another corridor. Even as she does so, she sees
TIFFANY disappearing again into yet another intersection.
KIRSTY follows and, again, the same thing happens.
This happens several times and, always, KIRSTY never quite loses sight of TIFFANY
but never quite catches up with her either.
In short, TIFFANY's instincts were absolutely right; this too is another puzzle. The girls
are lost in a concrete maze, full of twists and turns and labyrinthine windings.
After enough turns have been made to completely confuse KIRSTY's sense of direction,
she makes a final turn into one corridor and sees something different.
At the end of this corridor is a blinding white light. As soon as
KIRSTY sees the light, the air is filled with beautiful birdsong.
TIFFANY disappears into the light as soon as KIRSTY sees it.
Despite the light, despite the birdsong, KIRSTY is still suspicious and shouts out.

KIRSTY
Tiffany! Don't trust it! Don't
Trust it!
But it is too late. The girl is gone. KIRSTY follows-and vanishes into the light.

INT. CORRIDORS/LABYRINTH

JULIA and MALAHIDE are seen in the corridors of the labyrinth.

MALAHIDE's face is full of delight. He is absolutely the enchanted visitor.

JULIA, on the other hand, walks with the brisk assurance of one on familiar territory.

The corridors that MALAHIDE sees are different to KIRSTY'S; they are grotto-like, dotted with stalactites and stalagmites and not immediately unattractive. The walls contain portals of a glass- like substance at random intervals that emit blooming lights of different colors and MALAHIDE peers eagerly into several of these.

In one, the view is like an aquarium. An alien fish swims past his eyes. Its body resembles a human brain but it has pincer-like claws.

MALAHIDE presses his hand against the glass as the thing comes nearer.

Suddenly, from within its body, the thing produces a perfect human forearm and hand and meets MALAHIDE's hand on the other side of the glass.

MALAHIDE starts slightly but then keeps his hand there. He is turning his head to call JULIA's attention to this marvel when the thing suddenly forms a fist and begins to beat against the glass with tremendous force.

MALAHIDE jumps back sharply, but the thing shatters the glass and leaps out at him. He gasps and runs up the corridor, the thing hopping after him on its one hand.

As they pass JULIA, she tuts with the slightly exasperated but indulgent tone of a parent or a teacher. She steps on the thing, squashing it flat. It emits a horrible death-cry.

JULIA
Do be careful.

INT. HELL'S SITTING ROOM DAY
White light fills the screen and KIRSTY steps through it into view. Instantly the White light contracts and disappears.

KIRSTY finds herself standing in a beautiful family sitting room.

The room is bathed in the warm light of a perfect summer's day.

The birdsong KIRSTY heard earlier continues but is, if anything, even more melodic, even more sweet.

The room is vaguely Edwardian in its decor; real wood furnishings and decorative porcelain ornaments. There is a large wooden dresser, on top of which are many photographs in old-fashioned brass frames.

Despite herself, KIRSTY cannot resist a smile of pure pleasure at the appearance of the room.

She touches some of the furniture, as if to assure herself it is real.

She approaches the dresser and picks up one of the large framed photographs. She gasps in pleasure.

We see the photograph. It is a family group and looks to be have been taken ten to twenty years ago. It is of a man, a woman, and a young girl of four or five.

The man is clearly LARRY, albeit a younger version, and the little girl has dark, thick, slightly curly hair - just like

KIRSTY'S. The woman is beautiful and has similar hair to her daughter.

KIRSTY's eyes prick with tears - but they are clearly tears of happy memories. She smiles.

KIRSTY

Mommy...

KIRSTY puts down the photograph of her family and looks around the room again. A troubled look crosses her face.

Despite the aparent Summer light in the room, KIRSTY suddenly realises what it is that is odd.

She looks from wall to wall with mounting distress on her face.

There are no windows in the room. And no door.

At this point, the odd discordant note in the birdsong becomes apparent. It is nothing too obvious at the moment - the total effect is simply less sweet than it was.

KIRSTY looks back at the photograph and snatches it up, with a look of concern.

The photograph has changed. It is now a wedding photo. The wedding of LARRY and JULIA.

Suddenly the photograph begins to bleed. Blood pours from the paper itself, pressing up and smearing against the glass-so that it is momentarily framed blood, without a single trace of the picture showing. The blood begins to escape out of the frame, trickling over the lip that holds the glass in place and dripping onto KIRSTY's fingers. With a cry of horror, KIRSTY drops the frame. It lands on the floor and the glass shatters. The blood continues to flow. In fact, now that the glass does not restrain it, it fairly fountains out, spreading across the floor.

KIRSTY steps back and glances at the dresser. Blood is flowing from every frame, pooling on the dresser and overflowing onto the floor.

By now, the discordant elements in the birdsong are very much predominant and, as KIRSTY sweeps all the frames off the dresser and onto the floor with a scream of anguish, the birdsong gives way completely to a hideous, dissonant shrieking.

KIRSTY throws her hands to her ears.

KIRSTY

Nooooo!

She rushes at one of the walls and begins beating it with her fists.

The walls are soft and pulpy and give slightly as her fists strike, like flabby flesh. KIRSTY stands back in disgust.

The wall visibly bruises before her eyes, swelling and purpling.

The light in the room, like the birdsong, has changed utterly. It is not dark, but simply dull, featureless, and depressing.

KIRSTY turns away in disgust and finds that the whole room has given in to decay. The sofas and chairs are mildewed and rotten, the wooden furniture is ridden with woodworm and rot. A skinned rat runs across the room beside the buckled and chipped skirting board.

A rotten leg gives way under a small chest and the bottom drawer spills out, freeing a whole family of quite large spiders which run wildly across the floor.

Suddenly the room begins to fill with smoke, churned up by an ever-increasing intensity of wind. The smoke obscures the screen.

INT. BARE CHAMBER HELL

The smoke and wind subside but not entirely.

KIRSTY is standing in exactly the same position in a room of exactly the same proportions, but which is completely empty and which has walls of the same gray stone that the corridors do.
Suddenly, rising up from behind KIRSTY, comes PINHEAD.

PINHEAD
Ah, Kirsty. And we thought we'd lost you.
KIRSTY swings round in terror. As the mist continues to clear, she sees, advancing to join PINHEAD, the FEMALE CENOBITE and the
CHATTERER. Beyond them, it is now revealed, that this chamber has no fourth wall; it gives directly onto the corridors

FEMALE CENOBITE
So sweet of you to come back.
KIRSTY begins to work furiously at the BOX she has brought from
MALAHIDE's house. It sent them away at the end of HELLRAISER.
She obviously hopes it will work again.
PINHEAD raises a hand and the box simply flies out of KIRSTY's hands and hovers in the air between them. KIRSTY stares, open- mouthed.

PINHEAD
How can it send us back, child?
We're already here. And so are you.
Suddenly PINHEAD works at the box himself - by remote control and with dazzling skill.
He turns the box rapidly through positions KIRSTY and we have never seen before - even opening it out at one stage into a large, two-dimensional square. Finally, it closes itself down - but in a wholly new shape; a white, multi-faceted, diamond shape
- and drops back into KIRSTY's hands.
He stares at KIRSTY and makes a small gesture with his brow. It is ALMOST cute. If anything, it resembles the cocky, aren't-I- clever look STEVE gave KIRSTY after swallowing the cigarette in
HELLRAISER. Then his face assumes its normal deadly blankness.
KIRSTY shakes her head dumbly and begins to back into a corner, hoping that if they converge on her, she might just be able to slip around them and get back to the labyrinth.

KIRSTY
No! You... You can't! It wasn't me...I didn't do it! I didn't open the box!

FEMALE CENOBITE
Didn't open the box. And what was it last time? Didn't know what the box was. And yet we DO keep finding each other, don't we?

PINHEAD
Oh, Kirsty; so eager to play, so reluctant to admit it.

FEMALE CENOBITE
Perhaps you're teasing us. Are you teasing us?
To some extent, KIRSTY's ploy is working. The CENOBITES are moving closer together as they advance to the corner in which she stands.

KIRSTY
But I didn't open it! I didn't!

PINHEAD
Then why are you here?

KIRSTY
I've come for my father!
KIRSTY shouts this with brave defiance. PINHEAD laughs in response, a very unattractive sound.

PINHEAD
But he's in his own Hell, child
And quite unreachable.
Suddenly KIRSTY makes her break shouting out as she does so.

KIRSTY
I don't believe you!
It seems for a moment she has succeeded. She swings around the side of the CENOBITES and begins to run across the chamber.
The CENOBITES do not move but suddenly, from nowhere a hook flies across the room, attached to a metal chain. The hook buries itself in the wall only inches in front of KIRSTY's face, the chain pulled tight and barring her path. The wall begins to bleed. KIRSTY screams.
The CENOBITES turn to face her, but make no attempt to cross the room to her new position.

PINHEAD
But it's true, He is his own Hell.
Just as you are in yours.

KIRSTY
And what about you?
PINHEAD almost smiles at the naivete of the question.

PINHEAD
It's different for us.

FEMALE CENOBITE
We've always been here.

PINHEAD

We have no more surprises.
Suddenly, as quickly as it came, the hook withdraws from the wall and flies back into nothingness.
PINHEAD puts out his hand in an expansive gesture.

PINHEAD

But, please; feel free.
Explore. We'll always be here...

INT. CORRIDOR

KIRSTY can't quite believe this but she has no intention of questioning it. She runs into the corridor and away, with
PINHEAD's last words echoing after her.

PINHEAD

... we have Eternity to know your flesh!
Delighted CENOBITE laughter follows her back into the labyrinth.
KIRSTY drops the transformed BOX into her pocket as she begins running through the corridors again. The labyrinth seems tighter now - the corridors shorter, the turns sharper.
Corner after corner we see KIRSTY turn.
Accompanying this tightening, the light in the corridors becomes gradually murkier - not quite dark, more like the oppressive colourlessness that descends before a thunderstorm breaks.
Occasionally there are little hissing noises from the walls themselves, which are accompanied by small jets of dull and heavy smoke escaping between the bricks.
Over all this, there grows in volume on the soundtrack a rhythmic, labored, resonant sound - a sound somewhere between breathing and machinery.
Suddenly, as KIRSTY turns one more corner, a hand reaches out to touch her.
KIRSTY throws herself back against the far wall of the corridor, unsure whether to fight or flee. Then her face relaxes. It is

TIFFANY.

INT. CORRIDORS/LABYRINTH

In another corridor within the labyrinth, MALAHIDE and JULIA are walking.
They too have found their way into the inner sections. They too are in tighter, sharper corridors where the light is distressing.
They too hear the machine-like breathing noise. And what is revealed behind the portals in the corridor walls is less ambiguous in its unpleasantness; in one we see CHATTERER in some
Hell's equivalent of a beauty salon. He is being re-made. This involves the scar tissue being manually peeled from the upper part of his face to reveal beneath small, vicious, human eyes.
MALAHIDE's attitude has begun to change, as well. His nervousness now clearly outweighs his delight. He' rushes on to the next portal.

If the last room was a beauty salon, this is the orgy room. But the orgy is very strange. It is a very dark room, filled with a faint layer of smoke. In the background, a bound man is having his chest licked by a kneeling woman. She pulls her face back for a moment. Her tongue is horrifically long and studded with short, sharp blades. The man's chest is stripped of skin where she has been attending him. His face is a picture of ecstasy.

In the foreground, three people are buried up to their waists in the floor. They are naked. The one in the middle is a woman, the other two, men. The one in front of her faces her, the one behind has his back to her back. They are all very, close. The men have various hooks in their chests, connected by chains to the unseen walls and their faces are impassive. The woman is unwounded and her head flicks back and forth, as if in the grip of a sexual climax of stunning ferocity. The movements of her head keep the details of her features blurred until, finally, it turns to give

MALAHIDE a three-quarter profile and holds its position, its mouth open, its eyes half-closed in pleasure. It is JULIA's face.

MALAHIDE gasps and pulls back from the portal. The camera TRACKS back to reveal that JULIA is still in the corridor, just a few yards in front of him

JULIA

Come. I have such sights to show you.

MALAHIDE shakes his head crazily from side to side and begins to back away.

JULIA looks at him and walks toward him slowly. She smiles. She strokes his cheek. She moves closer, gently slipping her arms around him and molding her body to his. She extends her tongue and licks lightly at his lower lip. He opens his mouth and returns the kiss, pressing her body more firmly to him. The kiss becomes quite passionate.

INT. CORRIDORS/LABYRINTH

KIRSTY and TIFFANY are now walking together.

KIRSTY is talking to her as calmly as her sense of urgency will allow.

KIRSTY

Do you see? You were RIGHT.

This IS a puzzle, too. But

WE'RE CAUGHT in the puzzle.

KIRSTY stops walking and catches hold of TIFFANY's arm. TIFFANY stops, looks at the hand holding her arm, and then looks into

KIRSTY's eyes.

KIRSTY

Yeah?

TIFFANY smiles directly at KIRSTY and then returns her nod.

KIRSTY

Yeah?

TIFFANY nods again, more emphatically.

KIRSTY
Yeah!
KIRSTY throws her arms around TIFFANY and hugs her.

INT. CORRIDORS/LABYRINTH
JULIA is leading MALAHIDE down a corridor which has intersections every few yards
on both of its sides.
JULIA walks past these shadowed entrances without pause, without a single sidelong
glance. She is clearly confident, clearly back on her own turf.
MALAHIDE, on the other hand, glances nervously into every one before moving on.
There is also one last portal he looks into. He is gazing into a room where the floor is a
vast, seething pool of maggots.
Suddenly, something breaks the surface. It would doubtless scream were its mouth not
full of maggots. It is BROWNING. His nightmare has come true; his skin is producing
the maggots in a constant, spewing flow from numerous sores that pack his face.
MALAHIDE turns away and calls to JULIA.

MALAHIDE
Enough. God, that's enough. We
HAVE to go back.
JULIA smiles at him.

JULIA
Go back? What an earth makes you think we can go back?
MALAHIDE's jaw drops.

MALAHIDE
I want to go back!

JULIA
Sorry, friend. No day trips to
Hell. Here you are. Here you stay. And forward the only way to go.
JULIA turns back and walks an down the corridor.
MALAHIDE, with a glance back at the maggot pool, turns after the now departing
JULIA.

INT. CORRIDORS/LABYRINTH
KIRSTY and TIFFANY are walking warily along a corridor when, suddenly, the
corridor wall parts with a roar. Both girls jump, and TIFFANY cries out.
A new, and very narrow corridor has been revealed. The GIRLS stare down it. It
culminates in a door. Despite being set in a blank gray stone wall, the door is normal.
But frightening - because it is an exact replica of the front door of 55 LODOVICO
STREET, LARRY's house.
Before KIRSTY can react to this, a voice issues from beyond the door.

VOICE

Kirsty!
KIRSTY stops dead in her tracks. She looks at the door and moves toward it, walking
slowly down the corridor. TIFFANY follows.

KIRSTY
(Very Tentatively)
Daddy...?
Only a low moan comes from behind the door.

KIRSTY
Tiffany. Wait here. If I'm not back real soon - get out. Get home.
Leaving TIFFANY in the corridor, KIRSTY opens the door and steps in.

INT. THE BROTHERS' ROOM
The door that KIRSTY opens gives directly on to a room.
Like the SITTING ROOM earlier this appears to be an ordinary room and not a stone
wall chamber.
It's wall-papered walls were once white but are now yellowed and old. Overhead there
is an equally ancient four bladed wooden fan that turns sluggishly.
In the middle of the floor is a small low table of vaguely
Eastern design.
On this table lie a hand of cards, face down, an empty and cloudy tumbler, and a soiled
ashtray.
Over by the far wall (the wall opposite to that containing the door) there is a mattress
on the floor. A body like shape on this mattress is obscured by a heavy blanket that
covers it.
To the side of the mattress a latticed wooden screen stands, hiding whatever is behind
it from those entering the room. If the atmosphere of the room reminds us of anything
it is of the seedy bazaar where FRANK first bought the LAMENT CONFIGURATION.
We are looking at the door as it opens inwards and KIRSTY slowly and nervously walks
into the room.
KIRSTY advances into the room. She stares at the mattress ahead of her. Above it
written in blood on the wall, is the message she saw in her vision. I AM IN HELL:HELP
ME.

KIRSTY daddy...
A low moan comes from the far end of the room. KIRSTY assumes it issues from the
figure hidden beneath the blanket and walks nearer, lifting her arm in readiness to
remove the blanket.

KIRSTY
Daddy. It's Kirsty...
There is no response. KIRSTY arrives at the mattress and pulls the blanket back. She
leaps backwards, her hand at her mouth stifling a scream.
Lying on the bed is a husk like figure, vaguely female in shape.

Despite its appearance of long decay, it is dressed in vaguely sexual garments of leather. Suddenly, the eyes pop open, revealing a vague remnant of life.

KIRSTY
Oh God.
KIRSTY hurriedly, throws the blanket back over it.
A voice issues into the room. It sounds like LARRY but, as we shall see, it is not.

VOICE
No. Over here. Behind the screen.
KIRSTY walks carefully around the screen, giving it a wide berth in case of a trick. There is a figure standing against the wall behind the screen. It is deeply shadowed by the screen itself but is clearly male.
KIRSTY gulps back a sob and her eyes fill with tears.

KIRSTY
Daddy... ?
The figure leans slowly into the light, speaking as he does so.

FRANK
That's it, baby. Come to
Daddy.
KIRSTY stands still. There is a second where her face registers nothing. Then she screams.

KIRSTY
NO! it is her UNCLE FRANK, back in his skin and dressed in white shirt and jeans.
FRANK chuckles. KIRSTY backs away from him into the room. FRANK puts out his right hand in a placatory gesture. KIRSTY realises he is not moving after her. She also sees that his body is curiously angled, the left side still in the deep shadow cast by the screen. Is there something else there? Something she can't quite see? FRANK's voice stops her wondering.

FRANK
What's the matter, Kirsty?
It's only Frank. It's only
Uncle Frank.
KIRSTY's anger at being tricked wins over her fear and distress and she shouts at FRANK in fury.

KIRSTY
I should have known! I should've known he wouldn't be here! This place is only for filth like you!
FRANK sneers.

FRANK

Oh, right. Daddy's died and gone to heaven, eh?

KIRSTY
Yes!

FRANK
Shit. Bull. Shit
FRANK pauses and smiles. Then he begins to move more fully into the room, shifting his weight as he does so and dragging what was hidden into the light. KIRSTY screams again.
FRANK's white shirt is cut off at the left shoulder. His arm is bare and, from the elbow down to the wrist, joined to another forearm. The flesh is completely fused, like that of siamese twins. As FRANK moves into the room, the owner of the other arm is revealed. It is his brother, LARRY. KIRSTY's father.
LARRY, like his brother, is dressed in a white shirt (cut off at one shoulder) and jeans and, like his brother, has his skin back.
His face is frozen into a permanent expression of terror and he seems incapable of any independent movement, simply being pulled along by FRANK.
KIRSTY steps back in horror.

FRANK
See? He's here. You should learn to believe your Uncle Frank.

KIRSTY
No! He SHOULDN'T be here! It
SHOULD'VE been a trick!

FRANK
'Fraid not, baby. He belongs here.
With me. We're the same. Brothers.
Equal and opposite. Pure appetite.
Pure banality. Too much feeling.
None at all.
KIRSTY's fear of FRANK is now outweighed by her contempt for his argument.

KIRSTY
You're full of shit, Frank Cotton.
My Dad wasn't like that at all.
He could feel. He could love. He loved ME.
KIRSTY's voice breaks.

KIRSTY
He...he loved me.

FRANK
Don't waste your tears. Look at him!

Her hatred for FRANK gives KIRSTY her strength back.

KIRSTY
He loved me, you bastard! He
Loved me, he loved my mother.
He even loved that bitch you betrayed him with!
FRANK begins to move towards KIRSTY again, LARRY dragging behind him.

FRANK
Ah, Julia. She hasn't been to see me recently. That's why it's so nice to have you here, baby. Daddy's little girl.
So pretty when she's upset. Come to Daddy,
FRANK is very close to her, now. KIRSTY attempts to run across the room. FRANK siezes her arm and throws her back against the wall. He moves in close and presses against her. His voice is midway between arousal and anger.

FRANK
Now don't be naughty, Kirsty. Or
I'll have to punish you first.
Perhaps you'd like that. Would you like that?
KIRSTY screams and stares pleadingly, at the still frozen LARRY.

KIRSTY
Daddy! Daddy! I love you! Help me!

FRANK
I'm your Daddy now, Kirsty.
FRANK leans in to kiss the terrified KIRSTY.
Suddenly, a hand appears at FRANK's throat and hurls him off
KIRSTY. It is LARRY, roused by his daughter's cries.

LARRY
Get your fucking hands off my daughter, you bastard!
Suddenly, the room, previously full of slow movements and tension, is full of furious, violent action as the fused brothers kick, tear, and punch at each other in a paroxysm of killing hatred.

INT. THE CENTRE OF HELL
MALAHIDE and JULIA are at the end of a corridor. They turn into an open space. A vast open space. It is desert-like in its expanse, almost vanishing into infinity at its furthest reaches.
It is criss-crossed by catwalks, on one of which MALAHIDE and
JULIA now stand. Beside these catwalks, the ground falls away into mile-deep, dark, abysses.
Above the catwalks, dominating the huge space, is the master of the labyrinth.

The master, LEVIATHAN, is a monumentally huge, white, multi- faceted diamond, spinning on its own axis, entirely unsupported by any physical means, above its territory.

Apart from its very immensity, the most unsettling thing about LEVIATHAN are the beams of black light that shine out from the corners of all its many facets. Due to the fast spinning, these beams shoot and swoop around the chamber, like a negative laser display of dazzling complexity.

The sound that has been in the corridors is now magnified. It is the sound of LEVIATHAN's breath.

MALAHIDE has walked the last few yards like a man in shock. Now a black beam strikes his face and images of horror flash before his eyes at almost subliminal speed. His face suddenly crumbles into an expression of incredulous terror, he makes a noise halfway between screaming and retching, and drops to his knees by the edge of the catwalk.

Unfortunately, this allows him to look down into LEVIATHAN's pit.

Looking down with him, we are given a sudden and vertiginously sickening realization of Hell's immensities. There is a drop of miles visible down the pit and, all the way down, as far as the eye can see, there are other catwalks cutting across the pit at various angles.

MALAHIDE looks back up, his scream renewed by his sight of the pit. Two or three of the beams of black light flit across his face, filling his eyes with more subliminal images of horror as they pass; a child, a knife, and a dead animal; a naked woman whose private parts are made of sharp, oily, metal; perfect hands ending in crumbling, leprous fingers. Suddenly, LEVIATHAN stops spinning. Effortlessly. Instantly. Two more beams are projected at MALAHIDE but, as they come within a few yards of him, they become writhing pink limbs that fly out, sieze MALAHIDE and lift him into the air. He screams out.

MALAHIDE
No! No! Julia! Help me!
MALAHIDE is held in the air as JULIA replies.

JULIA
But you WANTED this. You wanted to SEE. You wanted to KNOW. And here it is. The heart of Hell.
Leviathan.
As she says this two of the thing's facets part to reveal a raw and gaping cavity lined with angry, sore-looking purple flesh directly behind the dangling MALAHIDE.
The purple and pink walls of this flesh gash peel apart and open in various places to reveal blades, hooks and needles at the end of various vestigial limbs.
The limbs holding MALAHIDE draw him back inexorably into this cavity.
He has one last moment to meet JULIA's eyes.

JULIA
Why do you think I was allowed to go back? For YOU? No, it wanted souls. And I brought you.

And you wanted to KNOW. Now you're both happy.

MALAHIDE is now held within the walls of the gash. He opens his mouth for one final scream but one of the tiny needle-topped limbs flies at his mouth and sews his lips together with heavy blue wire before he can utter it.

His eyes widen in both agony and horror.

JULIA smiles.

JULIA

Goodbye, Doctor. It's been real.

The gash heals itself, closing MALAHIDE within.

Despite the gash having closed over MALAHIDE, the leathery flesh that covers that area is a mass of movement, ripples and bumps.

Small rips and gashes appear and disappear on its surface, allowing us occasional and partial glimpses of MALAHIDE and what is happening to him.

At one stage MALAHIDE's hand and forearm appear. A long deep, running cut has been made down the arm and the flesh peeled and folded back, revealing the meat and the muscle beneath. As we watch, two of the tiny operating limbs sew the flaps of flesh, still folded back, to the rest of the arm, leaving the wound open and un-healable.

Another gash opens and MALAHIDE's face is visible. Here too the needles are at work, diving into and out of his flesh in a complicated sewing pattern that is finally pulled together beneath one ear, leaving MALAHIDE's features permanently pulled out of shape and decorated with running stitches of metal wire.

Again, MALAHIDE's torso appears, naked. Two large triangular blades make deep parallel slashes down his chest. Two different limbs appear but these have sucker-like tips rather than metallic ones. They fasten onto the new cuts, as if battening. Instead they are injecting - as becomes apparent when MALAHIDE's skin turns blue.

The blueness, the conscious disfigurement, and the almost decorative open wounds should serve to convey that what is happening to MALAHIDE is not simply torture; he is being transformed into a CENOBITE.

JULIA watches with avid interest.

INT. BROTHERS' ROOM

LARRY and FRANK are fighting furiously, tumbling around the room. LARRY is fuelled by righteous anger and revenge but FRANK has had more experience of dirty fighting.

At one stage their free hands each have hold of the other man by the throat and are rolling along one of the walls, each trying to establish the dominant grip.

They smash violently against one of the walls in the room. It gives and they fall through into the next room.

INT. KNIFE ROOM

This is a small square room. With the exception of the doorway to the BROTHERS ROOM, every inch of the walls is covered with sharp and deadly-looking double-bladed knives -ie One blade is buried in the wall up to a central hilt/handle and the other blade juts out menacingly into the room.

The two brothers tumble into the room. Their grips loosened by their fall through the wall, they land on the floor and rise to their feet, staring at each other but taking in the vicious nature of the room as well.

FRANK
How convenient.
KIRSTY comes through and gasps as she sees the walls.

LARRY
Stay there, baby. Don't come in.

FRANK
Yes. Stay there. I'll be with you in a minute.
LARRY and FRANK trade blows.
FRANK lands a powerful blow to LARRY's jaw. It straightens LARRY up and FRANK slams the flat of his hand against his brother's chest.
LARRY flies backwards. He flings out his arm to balance himself but he is nearer to the wall than he thinks and the impetus of his fall drives his arm onto the knives.
LARRY cries out. FRANK grins and prepares to force his wounded brother completely onto the knives.
Suddenly KIRSTY flies across the room at FRANK and beats at his back with her fists. FRANK snarls and, without turning around completely, flings her away from him. KIRSTY goes flying but lands just safely short of the deadly walls.
LARRY, in the pause KIRSTY gave him and galvanized by her example, has found more strength. He pulls his arm painfully forward, clear of the knives, and throws himself to the side, forcing FRANK onto the knives. With a vicious push, LARRY impales his brother completely.
FRANK howls, loud and long.
Without pausing, LARRY pulls a knife free from the wall and, with one vicious slice, separates himself from his brother.
LARRY rushes to KIRSTY and helps her to her feet. They embrace.
There is a cry of horror off-camera. We pull out. TIFFANY has followed her friend. She stares in shock at LARRY's wounded arm and at the impaled FRANK.

INT. THE CENTRE OF HELL
JULIA is being given more glimpses of the transforming MALAHIDE.
The major surgery seems to be complete. There are no spinning blades of needles in sight as the gashes open. MALAHIDE's head is completely bald and his face, like the rest of his skin is blue.
The only new sophistications are that his upper and lower eyelids have been stretched wide and stapled to his face and forehead, and that a new mouth has been sliced into what was his cheek before his features were pulled permanently to one side.
Over the sound of LEVIATHAN's breath and the CENOBITE machinery still at work on MALAHIDE, FRANK's howl is heard.
JULIA's head turns to the direction of this new sound.

JULIA
Frank...
She turns away without a backward glance and moves back into the corridors.

INT. THE KNIFE ROOM
FRANK is still impaled on the knives, but his anguished howl has
Become small whimpers of complaint (with, given his history with the CENOBITES,
perhaps the tiniest note of pleasure in there, too)
KIRSTY, LARRY and TIFFANY are now gathered together to one side of the room
near the door that leads to the corridor. They should leave, but a kind of sick fascination
keeps them watching FRANK.
FRANK realises only leverage will pull him free of the knives and lifts his forearms up
as much as they are free to.
He turns his palms to face the knives and, with a growl of self- encouragement, drives
them deeply onto the knives so that he can begin to push the rest of his impaled body
backwards.
It takes several seconds and much pain for him to succeed, but succeed he does. He
flops backwards into the room.
Several of the knives have stayed in him, rather than the wall - his chest is decorated,
or armed, with many blades.
Just as FRANK begins to stand, and just as LARRY and the girls snap out of it and are
about to leave, the door from the CONVEYOR
BELT ROOM opens and JULIA walks into the room.
KIRSTY and LARRY gasp. FRANK gives a slow smile.

JULIA
Well, well. All my family together again. How very sweet.

FRANK
(delighted/flattered)
Julia.

JULIA
(Flatly)
Frank.

FRANK
I knew you'd come.

JULIA
You knew?

FRANK
Yes. You're a girl who remembers her promises.

JULIA

Oh, I do. I do.
FRANK grins, his grin taking in LARRY, KIRSTY and TIFFANY as well as JULIA.
He extends an arm to JULIA.

FRANK
And I know how much I mean to you. Come here.
JULIA does not move.

FRANK
Come here. Kiss me. And then...
He glances meaningfully at the others, perhaps stroking a blade of one of the knives in
his chest.

FRANK
... we'll have a real family re-union.
Suddenly, surprisingly, LARRY laughs. He is genuinely amused.

LARRY
Jesus Christ, FRANK. I don't believe you. You don't know her at all do you? You still
think you're in charge.
JULIA still has not moved.

FRANK
Of course I am. She BELONGS to me.
JULIA begins to cross the room to him.

KIRSTY
For God's sake! He KILLED you!
JULIA doesn't pause. FRANK grins.

FRANK
She's forgiven me that. Haven't you?
JULIA is now next to him.

JULIA
Do you really need to ask?
FRANK laughs.

FRANK
Show them.
JULIA glances at the knives. FRANK shrugs.

FRANK
Just a small inconvenience, babe.

JULIA shifts position so she is standing behind him. She wraps her arms around him, one stroking his belly, the other across his shoulders. FRANK leans his head back and twists it slightly.

They kiss.

JULIA removes her arm from his stomach and slips it behind him.

Nothing happens for a second and then, suddenly, FRANK's whole body spasms. We almost think it may be with pleasure until he breaks from the kiss and we see the confused expression on his face - and the blood bubbling at his mouth.

There is a ripping, bursting sound and JULIA's hand emerges from his chest, covered in his blood. Clutched in her hand is his ruptured, still pumping heart.

LARRY
Jesus! Out. Out!
He shepherds the girls quickly through the door to the corridor.
FRANK's body begins to twitch. JULIA holds it tightly.

INT CORRIDORS/LABYRINTH
They reach the end of the corridor. It terminates in a T- junction.
TIFFANY automatically heads in one direction. KIRSTY makes to follow, but LARRY hesitates.

LARRY
Wait a minute. Why are we following her? Who is this?

KIRSTY
This is Tiffany
KIRSTY shrugs.

KIRSTY
... She's good at puzzles.

LARRY
Fine.
They take the turn TIFFANY has indicated.

INT THE KNIFE ROOM
JULIA still holds FRANK tight.
Slowly, she raises the hand which holds his heart until it is in front of his face. FRANK's eyes are glassing over but he can still see.

JULIA
Nothing personal, babe.
Without ceremony, she bursts the heart with one quick squeeze.

INT THE CENTRE OF HELL
LARRY, KIRSTY and TIFFANY come running toward the camera.

Initially oblivious to the fact that the corridor they were running along has widened and the walls retreated. Suddenly, they come to a stunned halt together, staring ahead of them with awestruck faces.

KIRSTY
Oh. My. God.
The camera moves around them to take in what they see. They are of course in the central chamber of LEVIATHAN.
LEVIATHAN is spinning again, the black beams flying around the chamber.
TIFFANY screams. KIRSTY grabs her.

KIRSTY
Tiffany, listen. You've solved it. But we've got to solve it the OTHER way. See? See? We've got to get out.
TIFFANY is frozen.

LARRY
Come on!
LEVIATHAN spins, the beams fly.

KIRSTY
Please! Tiffany, Please!
Get us out! Take us home, please!
TIFFANY nods. They are just about to leave when LEVIATHAN stops spinning.
A large beam flies down , carrying an object which lands on the catwalk before the HUMANS, who all take a step or two backwards.
The beam withdraws.
The object at first resembles a large and bloody plastic bag, but then internal movement begins to rip at this covering. Hands appear out of the rips and complete the removal. We realise that the bag-like thing was a kind of caul, a membranous after-birth that some creatures produce their young in.
The thing inside completes its escape and stands clear of the shredded caul. Like a new-born child, it is stained and soiled with amiotic fluids and blood. But it is not a new born child.
It is a NEW CENOBITE. And it used to be MALAHIDE. The transformation we caught glimpses of is now complete. Its skin is entirely blue, its head entirely bald. The decorative wounds and tortures we saw being applied are all present; its flesh is peeled back in various places, its features are threaded and distorted by, wire, its eyelids are stapled open.
For a second it stands and regards the HUMANS before it.
TIFFANY gasps in recognition.
KIRSTY too knows what it was.

KIRSTY
Malahide ...

For some reason, KIRSTY draws from her pocket the photo she took from the OBSESSION ROOM. She stares at it.

KIRSTY
Jesus Christ! Of course ...
The MALAHIDE CENOBITE stretches its arms and flexes its fingers.

MALAHIDE
And to think I hesitated ...
It looks at the HUMANS again, its gaze finally settling on the still shocked TIFFANY.

MALAHIDE
Tiffany. Come. I have a whole new world of puzzles for you to enjoy ...
It reaches out its hand to her.

MALAHIDE
A whole new world of pleasures for you to endure.
TIFFANY, confused and used to obeying her doctor's voice, tentatively stretches out her arm to meet the MALAHIDE
CENOBITE's.
LARRY suddenly walks between TIFFANY and MALAHIDE. The expression on his face is strange; it is not fear, nor defiance.
It is simpler than that. He is really, really pissed off.

LARRY
No. I've had enough of this shit.
Who the hell are you?

KIRSTY
It's ...
LARRY waves a hand at her, but keeps his eyes on

MALAHIDE.
LARRY
Never mind. Never mind.
He points a finger at MALAHIDE's face, which is attempting a version of PINHEAD's imposing glacial stars, but frankly, isn't quite making it.

LARRY
Fuck you and the horse you rode in on.
Suddenly, he forms a fist with his unwounded arm and smashes it straight into MALAHIDE's face. MALAHIDE is completely decked.
LARRY grabs TIFFANY by the shoulders and speaks urgently to her.

LARRY
O.K. You've done it before. You can do it again. GET US OUT OF

HERE!

The three of them run back up the catwalk.

LEVIATHAN spins wildly and a myriad of black beams flow from it.

As they shine into the catwalk they become limbs like those that captured MALAHIDE, but all with different tips; some are organic, vicious mouths, some are hooks or blades, some are faces, some are (as if LEVIATHAN Is too angry to be thinking straight) beautiful flowers.

The limbs fly up the catwalk, but the HUMANS have gained too great a start. The limbs retract rapidly into the black lights.

MALAHIDE staggers to his feet, just as LEVIATHAN re-directs its energy into forming and projecting one much fatter limb. It is dirty pink and segmented, like a vast earthworm. The end peels back as it flies toward MALAHIDE, revealing a cruel, metallic, and rapidly-spinning surgical saw.

Just as MALAHIDE stands up straight, the limb smashes into the back of his skull. There is a distressing WHIRRING noise as the limb seals itself fleshily to MALAHIDE's skull and the former surgeon twitches and dances in horrible involuntary movements as

LEVIATHAN takes over what little mind remains.

INT CORRIDORS/LABYRINTH

KIRSTY, TIFFANY and LARRY are running, TIFFANY making the decisions as to direction.

Down one corridor, blades and knives jut out from the opposite walls at random intervals and they have to weave at high speed between them. They negotiate the corridor successfully but, just as KIRSTY, bringing up the rear, emerges from it, she stumbles and half-falls. The re-structured BOX falls from her pocket and rolls back a few feet up the corridor.

TIFFANY, who is nearest to her, helps her to her feet and, as she does so, catches sight of the BOX (or white diamond, as it is now). She makes as it to go and get it. KIRSTY holds her arm.

KIRSTY

No. Come on. We have to get out of here.

TIFFANY moves away with KIRSTY, but not without a backward glance and a puzzled expression.

They all make another turning. Suddenly, when they are about halfway down this next corridor, a new gap opens up behind them in the wall and a terrible sucking noise is heard. Corridor debris disappears into the vacuum.

Luckily, LARRY has reached the end of the corridor and grasps the corner with one hand, seizing KIRSTY's hand with the other.

KIRSTY grabs TIFFANY and the three of them flatten themselves against the wall, fighting against the suction. The force is tremendous and LARRY's finger are slowly losing hold.

INT. CORRIDORS/LABYRINTH

CLOSE UP on a hand picking up the re-structured BOX from the corridor floor they have just left.

INT. CORRIDORS/LABYRINTH
The sucking force is growing stronger by the second. Not only is
LARRY's right hand losing its grip on the edge of the wall, but his left arm - stretched tight as it clings to KIRSTY and, via her, TIFFANY - is bleeding profusely again.
Suddenly, JULIA appears at the top of the corridor next to LARRY.
In her hand is the white diamond BOX that KIRSTY had let drop.
She stays just out of range of the sucking wind. She stares at
LARRY's weakening fingers and smiles.

JULIA
Oh, poor Larry. You never could hold on to anything for very long, could you?
Suddenly, audaciously, his face set in a scowl of anger, LARRY lets go of the wall.
Before she realises what is happening, he has grabbed JULIA's wrist and pulled her off her feet into the corridor. He lets go almost immediately and with a superhuman effort grabs at the corner again before the wind can claim him and the girls.
JULIA is not so lucky; without support or foothold, she is seized by the wind and hurtles to the gap in the wall.
She manages to brake herself by flinging her arms out to either side of her. For a moment she is hold there and then the pressure begins to draw her in.
In her left hand she still holds the BOX, but her right hand is only a few inches from TIFFANY's left.
TIFFANY reaches her hand to her, not knowing JULIA as the others do. Their fingers just manage to interlock when JULIA's face registers a disbelieving shock.
There is a terrible ripping sound. JULIA's new skin, so recently gained, is giving up its hold and has ripped right up the spine.
JULIA is drawn from it.

JULIA
NOOOOOOOOOOO!
With a final, slurping sound, the skinned woman slips from the skin and disappears down the new corridor.
The momentary break in tension allows LARRY to make one last effort. He rounds the corner and pulls the girls after him.
TIFFANY, finally, realising what has happened, screams in terror and disgust, especially when she looks at what she has brought round the corner in her hand. She drops JULIA's skin to the floor as the three of them scramble to their feet and begin to run again.
Still clutched in the skin's hollow fingers is the white diamond BOX.
As they turn another corner, they see, very far in the distance, a glimmer of light.
TIFFANY points excitedly.

KIRSTY
My God, it's her room!

LARRY

Let's go!

He starts urging the girls down the corridor - a long and very narrow one - but KIRSTY
shows some resistance.

KIRSTY

No. No, there's something wrong...

Before they can discuss it, a new rushing sound is heard. They look back.

Hurtling towards them is the ENGINEER from HELLRAISER.

TIFFANY screams.

LARRY

Jesus. O.K. No more arguments.

Just RUN!

They begin one last panic-fuelled run down the narrow corridor, the ENGINEER at
their heels.

The sequence is equivalent to KIRSTY's pursuit by the ENGINEER in
HELLRAISER, the twist here being that as they approach the entrance into TIFFANY's
room the walls of the corridor, already thin, begin to close together.

LARRY is bringing up the rear (the corridor is now so narrow only single file is
possible) and he can almost feel the ENGINEER'S breath on his neck.

LARRY

Go. Go. Go. Go. Go!!

Finally, almost impossibly, they reach the gap in the wall.

TIFFANY tumbles through, then KIRSTY, and finally LARRY. Less than a micro-
second after LARRY has made it, the walls seal themselves.

104 INT. TIFFANY'S ROOM (2nd VERSION) DAY

As we see clearly the room they have come into, we perhaps share the feeling that
KIRSTY expressed in the corridor; Something Is
Wrong.

The tiles that make up the floor are patterned as before but the individual tiles are larger.
The room itself seems more spacious, the ceiling higher.

There is a bowl of flowers by the window. The flowers were in full bloom before their
trip to Hell but now they seem long dead.

The audience have to notice most of this for themselves because
LARRY, KIRSTY, and TIFFANY are too relieved by, and tired from, their escape to
take this in immediately. LARRY seats himself in the chair, KIRSTY perches on the
end of TIFFANY's bed. TIFFANY however walks straight across to her window. She
is the first to notice anything. She stares at the flowers.

KIRSTY

Tiffany ... ?

KIRSTY rises from the bed and joins TIFFANY by the window.

KIRSTY

But these were ... Daddy?

LARRY rises to his feet. Just as he stands, a fleeting expression of bewilderment crosses his face. He strokes at his right arm with an unconscious gesture as he crosses the room. KIRSTY doesn't look at her father right away.

KIRSTY

These flowers. I saw them just...

She looks at her father. A sea of sweat has broken out on his brow and face as he stares intensely at the flowers. KIRSTY's voice slows, begins to trail off.

KIRSTY

...the day ...before... yesterday

Daddy? Daddy!

LARRY's eyes close. His entire face screws up as if an excruciating pain just hit him. He clamps his arm across his chest, the hands clutching his shoulders. He opens his eyes and looks at KIRSTY for a second, his expression one of surprise.

Then his eyes roll up into the sockets and he collapses to the floor.

TIFFANY has hardly had time to turn from the bowl of flowers before KIRSTY is kneeling by her father.

KIRSTY

Daddy!

LARRY is unconscious. TIFFANY gasps. KIRSTY looks up at her.

KIRSTY

Get help.

TIFFANY's eyes widen. She rushes to the door and disappears into the corridor. Within two seconds we hear an emergency alarm go off and TIFFANY re-enters the room.

KIRSTY

Pass me a pillow.

TIFFANY does so and KIRSTY places it under the head of LARRY, whose lips are now blue and who is breathing very shallowly.

KIRSTY looks up at TIFFANY, despair in her eyes.

KIRSTY

What do you do? I just don't know what to do.

TIFFANY shakes her head helplessly.

Suddenly, the door to the room flies open and two INTERNS - maybe

Stan and Ollie from the carnival sequence - come in, complete with stretcher and gurney. They assess the situation with a glance and it is serious enough to make one of them break their professional silence.

INTERN

Coronary arrest. Let's be quick.

They are good at their job - within seconds LARRY is secured on the gurney and they head for the door, KIRSTY and TIFFANY behind them. The following exchanges are spoken on the move.

KIRSTY
Is he going to be O.K.?

INTERN
We just can't say.
O.R.'s on standby. They'll do what they can.

KIRSTY
But it's bad?
The INTERNS exchange a glance and decide honesty is best.

INTERN
(gently but flatly)
Yeah. It's bad.

INT. ELEVATOR DAY
The elevator is uncomfortably full, KIRSTY and TIFFANY squashed up against the back while the INTERNS hold the gurney in the centre.
The elevator is descending. The ride seems to take longer than it should, even though they are going to basement level;like the look of TIFFANY's room, it's ALMOST normal but just different enough to make us slightly uneasy in an un-focused way.
Eventually, though, it does come to a stop. TIFFANY squeezes
KIRSTY's shoulder sympathetically (NOTE. RE: TIFFANY's character
- it should be clear to the audience by this stage that, though she is still mute, TIFFANY is now a responsive, more rounded character)
The INTERNS wheel the gurney out of the elevator and the girls follow.

INT. BASEMENT CORRIDOR DAY
The basement corridor is long, cavernous, and not very pleasant.
It has a grimier, more uncared-for look than the upper floors and the high ceiling is covered with an intricate system of naked pipes and conduits.
The INTERNS wheel LARRY down this corridor, going so fast that
KIRSTY and TIFFANY are continually breaking into a trot to keep up with them.
At the far and of the corridor are a set of double doors. The nearer they all get to these doors, the tackier the corridor seems to become. The walls now have pipes running over them, as well as the ceiling, and several of these pipes are dripping water into small pools on the corridor floor. The sound of these drips is artificially loud on the soundtrack.
Finally, the doors are reached and the INTERNS, LARRY, KIRSTY and
TIFFANY disappear through them.

INT. PRE-OP ROOM DAY

This is a small ante-room to the operating room which is beyond a further set of double doors. Without ceremony the two INTERNS pass straight across this room to those doors and wheel the gurney through, one of them throwing back a parting remark to

KIRSTY.
INTERN
Wait out here. A doctor will talk to you when we know more.
The double doors part and close, giving just a glimpse of the operating room beyond, all lights, monitors and whirring machinery, and the several gowned and masked experts attending to LARRY.
As the doors close, KIRSTY turns to TIFFANY, expecting a long wait before anyone comes to speak to them. Surprisingly, though, the doors open again almost immediately and two figures step through. They, too, are masked and gowned in surgical green and very little of them is visible.

KIRSTY
Is he going to be all right?
1st GOWNED FIGURE
(matter of factly)
No. He's not going to be all right.
KIRSTY staggers visibly, shocked by this bluntness.

KIRSTY
Wh...
1st GOWNED FIGURE
No. He's going to die. He's got a ruptured aorta. He's going to die in agony.
As he makes this speech, the mask of his colleague stains rapidly with blood, as if it is literally pouring from its mouth.
Simultaneously, his own mask is slowly pierced by a score of nails bursting through from beneath.
TIFFANY screams.
The 1st GOWNED FIGURE pulls the mask and cap away from its face -
It is PINHEAD. His colleague does the same. It is the FEMALE

CENOBITE.
KIRSTY
Oh, Fuck.
She's had too much experience with these two to hesitate. She grabs TIFFANY's arm and bursts through the double doors to the corridor.

INT. BASEMENT CORRIDOR DAY
We are now looking along the corridor in the other direction - back towards the elevator.
KIRSTY and TIFFANY come into shot, running rapidly along the corridor.
As they make their way, a rumbling, flatulent sound is heard from the overhead pipes and they all begin to drip blood not water.
We hear the sound of the doors flying open behind them.

KIRSTY and TIFFANY reach the elevator. KIRSTY presses frantically on the call button, while TIFFANY looks behind them with frightened eyes.

KIRSTY
C'mon. C'MON!
The sound of steadily-pacing, purposeful feet is heard coming up the corridor, getting louder, coming closer.
KIRSTY begins hammering on the closed elevator doors. TIFFANY stifles a cry with her hand.

KIRSTY
COME ON!!
Suddenly, the doors fly open. KIRSTY and TIFFANY tumble into the elevator.

INT. BASEMENT CORRIDOR DAY (GIRLS' P.O.V.)
We see the door-frame of the elevator and the floor buttons beside it and, looking down the corridor through the open elevator doors, PINHEAD and the FEMALE CENOBITE marching towards us.
We also see KIRSTY'S finger jabbing frantically at the floor buttons. The doors are not closing. The CENOBITES are getting very close.
Finally, just as PINHEAD breaks from his determined but medium- paced stride and speeds up eagerly for the last two or three yards, extending his arm as he does so, the door slams shut across our vision and we hear the elevator machinery start up.

INT. ELEVATOR DAY
KIRSTY leans against the back wall of the elevator, breathing heavily. TIFFANY stands very still in the middle, a frozen expression of fear on her face.

KIRSTY
Faster, you bastard, faster!
She slams her fist against the elevator wall. The elevator stops. Its lights flicker.

KIRSTY
Oh, Jesus. I'm sorry. I'm sorry. I didn't mean it.
The elevator starts again.

KIRSTY
It's O.K. They can't beat an elevator. Not upstairs. It'll be O.K.
The lift stops, but this time it's where they want it. KIRSTY's finger hesitates over the DOOR OPEN button.

KIRSTY
It'll be O.K.
She presses the button.

INT. HOSPITAL CORRIDOR DAY (GIRLS P.O.V.)

We are looking at the closed elevator door. When it opens we will be looking down the corridor on the main hospital floor - the floor with the girls' rooms on.
The door flies open. CHATTERER II lunges in at them.
KIRSTY screams, but because of the eagerness of his lunge they are able to get around him as his impetus carries him to the back of the elevator.

INT. HOSPITAL CORRIDOR DAY
The door begins to close as the girls straighten up in the corridor and as CHATTERER II turns around to come back out at them.
He tries to put his hand out to stop the door closing, but succeeds only in trapping his fingers in the door.
KIRSTY, as soon as the doors began to close, had hit the DOWN button. Now, she squeals with horror as she realises what is about to happen.
The elevator begins to descend - we can tell this because
CHATTERER II's fingers move down to the floor and are then sliced off.
The GIRLS run off down the corridor.

KIRSTY
This way. Short cut.
They turn into a set of double doors leading to a large ward.

INT. LARGE WARD DAY
KIRSTY and TIFFANY enter the ward at a run and then slow down to a confused and horrified walk.
Every bed in the ward is occupied, some by men, some by women, and every patient has in their hands, and is busily working on, a

LAMENT CONFIGURATION.
Despite this collective work-in, the BOXES obviously still have the vicious characteristics they have previously demonstrated when used individually - as is witnessed by the ten or so patients who are struggling on with their work despite having one or two hooks and chains connecting their flesh to their BOX.
KIRSTY and TIFFANY move slowly down the room, a look of incredulity on both their faces.

KIRSTY
Oh, Christ. This isn't just personal anymore.
TIFFANY nods slowly, her eyes flicking back and forth across the ward.
Suddenly, the wheelchair patient from the earlier scene in this ward, who has been between two of the beds on one side of the ward, cuts across the GIRLS' path. He too has a BOX on his lap. As he passes in front of them, he looks at them, giggles in an unmistakably insane fashion, and gives them a conspiratorial wink. Then he simply proceeds to the other side of the ward.
A second or so after this, as the GIRLS edge down the middle of the room, they hear a rushing sound behind the double doors they are heading towards.
Suddenly, the doors slam open and revealed in the doorway is

MALAHIDE.
But he is not standing there. He is hovering about two feet off the floor. The umbilical limb that connects him to LEVIATHAN is still at the back of his skull. His face is contorted in a grin of manic glee as he floats three or four feet into the ward.

MALAHIDE
The Doctor is in!
He laughs, and the sound is far from human. KIRSTY and TIFFANY stare at him.

TIFFANY
Oh, shit.
KIRSTY looks sharply at TIFFANY for a second, as if she is about to comment on her re-found voice, but instead simply nods. She takes her friend's hand and the GIRLS begin to walk very slowly backwards to the far end of the ward.
MALAHIDE is too enraptured of his new power to pay attention to specific victims and so makes no move to stop the GIRLS' slow retreat.
Suddenly his palms erupt into a writhing mass of tentacle-like limbs as his head tips back to emit a wide band of LEVIATHAN's black light at the ceiling, accompanied by, renewed inhuman laughter.
Taking this as their cue, the GIRLS turn and bolt for the doors at the far and of the ward and exit through them.
The limbs extrude from MALAHIDE's palms only twelve inches or so and are all quite thin, but they all have independent movement and they all have various surgical-like, gleaming tips. MALAHIDE floats over to the nearest bed. He looks at the patient and then looks at the bladed tips of his new limbs and, as if addressing them, speaks.

MALAHIDE
I recommend amputation.
There is another burst of laughter as the limbs fly at the patient, writhing, twitching, slashing, and slicing.

INT. HOSPITAL CORRIDOR DAY
The GIRLS run wildly along the corridor, not knowing MALAHIDE is working his way through his former patients. They come to another door and pause. They look back down the corridor to ensure they are not visible as they hide and KIRSTY pushes the door open with the flat of her hand behind her. Carefully, still looking down the corridor, they back into the room and let the door close.

INT. HOSPITAL/TORTURE ROOM DAY
CLOSE UP on the GIRLS' faces as the door closes in front of them.
KIRSTY lets out a breath. Then they hear the rattling sound behind them. They swing round and the camera pulls out to take in the room.
It is like the TORTURE ROOM in HELLRAISER. The walls are black, the floor slimy, and the room filled with chains, hooks, and torture-pillars. And, in the room and staring at the GIRLS, are the four CENOBITES.

PINHEAD glances theatrically around the room, as if checking something.

PINHEAD
Oh. No Boxes. Such a shame.

FEMALE CENOBITE
No more delays, Kirsty. No more teasing. Time to play.

PINHEAD
Time to play.
KIRSTY looks at his unforgiving face and then her eyes suddenly widen as she thinks
Of something.

KIRSTY
Wait!

PINHEAD
No more deals, Kirsty. It's your flesh we want to experience, not your skill at bargaining.

KIRSTY
No deals! Just information.
Information. Free of charge.
No strings. Just information.

PINHEAD
Go on. But trick us again, child, and your suffering will be legendary even in Hell.
Carefully, making no fast movements, KIRSTY reaches into her pocket where she
placed the photograph from MALAHIDE's OBSESSION
ROOM. She brings out the picture that she realized earlier was of PINHEAD and hands
it to him.
He takes hold of it and looks, his face registering nothing.

PINHEAD
What is this? Someone else you think escaped us, like
Frank?

KIRSTY
No, No, this one didn't escape.
You told me you'd always been in Hell. You were wrong. Look at it. LOOK. IT'S YOU.

PINHEAD
Nonsense, I...

KIRSTY
It's you! You HAVEN'T always been as you are. You were
HUMAN. Remember. Remember all your confusions. Think!

The FEMALE CENOBITE strides across the room.

FEMALE CENOBITE
Enough!
She raises her hand towards KIRSTY. PINHEAD's arm flies out and stops her.

PINHEAD
Wait!
He is staring at the photograph, that great immobile brow finally puckering, as if something is stirring.

PINHEAD
I...remember.

KIRSTY
You were ALL human!
The other three CENOBITES stop moving and stare at KIRSTY. Any advances they were making on KIRSTY or TIFFANY stop as the same dim, distant, recollection begins to stir within them.
Suddenly, the door bursts open. MALAHIDE is there, still floating, his voice still a mixture of hideous threat and insane joy.

MALAHIDE
Tiffany. Come.
He turns his palms downwards, mirroring his gesture in the hall of mirrors.
TIFFANY lets out a moan of terror and shakes her head.
One of the snake-like limbs from MALAHIDE's palms flies towards
TIFFANY's face. Before anybody can react, its scalpel tip has sliced an inch or so off several strands of her hair.

MALAHIDE
Tiffany. Come.
KIRSTY throws her arms around the cowering TIFFANY and snarls at her tormentor.

KIRSTY
Leave her alone, you asshole!
MALAHIDE makes no reply, but suddenly several more limbs fly towards the GIRLS and begin to weave in front of KIRSTY's face like snakes awaiting their moment.
At this stage, the camera CUTS TO the watching PINHEAD. He lets the photograph of his past life flutter to the floor.
MALAHIDE looks up at the tiny noise this makes and his eyes meet
PINHEAD'S. He turns more fully to face PINHEAD and the other
CENOBITES who are now standing with their leader, and a strange smile crosses his face

MALAHIDE

Oh,good. A fight.

Suddenly, the air is full of flying chains. MALAHIDE is hooked everywhere. It is like a high-speed version of FRANK's final re- capture in HELLRAISER. The chains start tugging almost instantly.

Is MALAHIDE about to be ripped apart?

With contemptuous, dismissive speed, the limbs that ooze from

MALAHIDE's palms have sliced the chains to pieces and, almost before we have time to realise that, three of them have lengthened, thickened, and hardened and have skewered the FEMALE

CENOBITE, CHATTERER II, and BUTTERBALL to the walls.

The three limbs detach themselves from MALAHIDE. The three

CENOBITES are all well above the floor, pinned and twitching like the rats in FRANK's attic.

As they die, they suddenly revert; there are three human corpses on the walls of the room. A woman, a fat man, and a little boy.

MALAHIDE smiles. Be looks at PINHEAD again and advances. Suddenly a heavy torture pillar smashes into him, knocking him slightly off-balance.

PINHEAD is backing across the room, weaving pillars in front of him as he moves. MALAHIDE moves forward, knocking them out of the way. As each pillar is knocked aside, PINHEAD's face is more and more human. Finally, when the face we see is nearly that of the

ENGLISH OFFICER from the opening, he turns his head slightly away from the advancing MALAHIDE and finds KIRSTY's eyes. A look passes between them. Understanding? Gratitude? Friendship?

Whatever emotion lies beneath it, it is clearly a cue and

KIRSTY and TIFFANY make a break for it, bursting through the door. Simultaneously to this, MALAHIDE and PINHEAD find each other's eyes a final time. For a second, everything is still then a single bladed limb flies across the space between them and neatly and calmly slices PINHEAD's throat open. The thin red line becomes a torrent of blood and the former lord of Hell falls dead at the feet of his successor.

INT. HOSPITAL CORRIDOR DAY

KIRSTY and TIFFANY burst out into the corridor and almost fall over the PATIENT IN THE WHEELCHAIR.

PATIENT

So what, girls? It's O.K. for an ego-trip but it doesn't got the job done.

Shaking their heads at the insanity, they run up the corridor.

TIFFANY looks slightly distracted and when she speaks it is half to herself.

TIFFANY

I have to go back. Or it'll never stop.

KIRSTY

(Confused)

What are you talking...

TIFFANY
(to herself)
I've got to finish it.

KIRSTY
Finish what?
Even as KIRSTY says this, TIFFANY has moved past her and is resuming her run down the corridor.

KIRSTY
Tiffany! Wait!
KIRSTY starts after her friend.
They turn back into the main section of the corridor that contains their own rooms, TIFFANY still four or five yards in front of

KIRSTY.
TIFFANY reaches her room. The door is open. She goes in. A second later, KIRSTY follows.

INT. TIFFANY'S ROOM DAY
KIRSTY enters the room. It is as we last saw it except that the walls have re-parted to give onto the corridors of Hell.
Carefully and slowly, KIRSTY moves across to the entrance and looks down it. She is rewarded with the sight of TIFFANY just disappearing at the far end of the first corridor. With a grimace, KIRSTY follows her in.

INT. CORRIDOR/LABYRINTH
TIFFANY's skill at finding her way through puzzles means the
GIRLS are soon in the murkier corridors close to the Centre.
Hell seems angrier now, steam is issuing in jets from the corridor walls, the cries of children are heard faintly on the soundtrack, LEVIATHAN's breathing is more dominant, perhaps the light is even pulsing in time with it.
KIRSTY is still several yards behind TIFFANY. TIFFANY takes a corner and is out of sight for a second or so . KIRSTY dashes around the corner to find TIFFANY staring with distress at something on the floor.
It is the skin ripped off JULIA by the vacuum tunnel earlier.

KIRSTY
Oh, gross.
TIFFANY bends down and retrieves the white diamond BOX from the empty fingers.

KIRSTY
What are you doing? What are WE doing?
TIFFANY looks at the BOX in her hand. When she speaks, it is not to KIRSTY but to herself.

TIFFANY
I can't do it here. I have to go to it.

INT. THE CENTRE OF HELL
LEVIATHAN spins and fires light in the centre, his machine-like breathing drowning all other sound. We are looking down the catwalk as KIRSTY and TIFFANY approach its edge.
The beams of black light wash across their faces, as they passed over MALAHIDE's in the earlier scene. Images of horror freeze momentarily before them and then pass on, only to be replaced by others.

TIFFANY
I'm scared.

KIRSTY
No. Don't let it. You've come this far.
The GIRLS press on. Whether LEVIATHAN is oblivious to their presence or simply doesn't consider them a threat, the beams stop striking the GIRLS' faces. Nevertheless, the mood remains ominous. The audience should feel something is about to happen.
They are six feet from the lip of the catwalk. TIFFANY kneels and, holding the white diamond BOX in front of her, begins to move her fingers over it. The music box tune begins to play as the BOX begins to move.
That 'something' that the audience was waiting to happen, suddenly does; MALAHIDE flies up from the abyss beside the catwalk. The vastness of the limb that seals him to LEVIATHAN is now directly apparent; instead of merging into black light, the limb itself trails through the air over the huge distance to
LEVIATHAN itself.
One of the limbs from MALAHIDE's palms flies out and knocks the
BOX from TIFFANY's hands. It rolls perilously close to the edge of the catwalk.
KIRSTY grabs TIFFANY and, dragging her to her feet, pulls her further back down the catwalk as MALAHIDE floats to a landing between them and the BOX.

MALAHIDE
Ah, girls. And how are we feeling today?
The blades on the end of his limbs twitch eagerly.

MALAHIDE
You have your whole lives behind you now.
The limbs fly forward. KIRSTY screams and both girls run up the catwalk.
About halfway back up, however, TIFFANY stops, turns around, and begins to walk back. KIRSTY calls out.

KIRSTY
Tiffany! No!

The camera stays with TIFFANY as she makes her way back. KIRSTY's voice stays on the soundtrack for a time, imploring her friend to turn back and then simply stops. This should be abrupt enough to make the audience notice but smooth enough to avoid their attention leaving TIFFANY.

MALAHIDE waits, happy to see a patient so keen on the knife.

Very slowly, TIFFANY moves forward, inch by slow inch. This is something she HAS to do; the expression on her face is not determination but terror. And MALAHIDE is very happy to encourage this.

MALAHIDE
Surgery is open, Tiffany.
What was today's agenda?
His scalpels flick in the air, making small slicing motions.

MALAHIDE
Ah, yes. Evisceration.
Still TIFFANY comes forward, closer and closer until she is surely close enough to be grabbed.
Suddenly, she is grabbed. But from behind, and by a human hand.
TIFFANY gasps, and turns to see who has seized her. She screams.
It is JULIA.
The limbs retract into MALAHIDE's palms. He smiles.

JULIA
Doctor. I've missed you.
JULIA, having presumably just replaced her skin, is not quite as perfect as before; there are bloody lines like scars beneath her ears and chin as if the skin required some adjustment before being put on.
JULIA moves forward, her left arm still holding TIFFANY, her smile returning MALAHIDE'S.

MALAHIDE
I knew you'd come back.

JULIA
I'm a girl who keeps her promises.
JULIA is right next to MALAHIDE now. Smoothly, she releases her grip on TIFFANY and embraces MALAHIDE sensuously. He returns the embrace. They kiss.
Unseen, TIFFANY moves to the edge of the catwalk and picks up the
BOX. Her fingers move over it, finding its solution. Suddenly,
LEVIATHAN's breath becomes a roar of anger and fear.
MALAHIDE breaks away from his kiss, his face a mixture of confusion and rage.
JULIA plants both hands in the middle of his chest and pushes. He falls over the lip of the catwalk but, almost before he drops from sight, he is suddenly pulled backwards through the air, screaming, as LEVIATHAN's limb retracts. JULIA jumps back. shouting.

JULIA
Do it, Tiffany! Do it!

TIFFANY's fingers fly over the BOX and suddenly we see what is happening. The mountain-like LEVIATHAN is following the movements of the small replica in TIFFANY's hands. As TIFFANY inverts the new configuration back towards a closed BOX, LEVIATHAN too is being twisted and turned. Being closed.

The whole centre of Hell shakes as if suffering a mild earthquake. JULIA and TIFFANY almost lose their footing, but

TIFFANY continues working. She is nearly, there. LEVIATHAN is halfway between its white diamond, majesty and a huge closed BOX.

TIFFANY takes her hands from the BOX. It is done. The larger BOX operates a few seconds behind it's control, so that we can inter- cut the final sliding and creaking into position with the following human drama;

As LEVIATHAN makes its final closing, the mild tremors of before become larger. Hell shakes violently and this time TIFFANY does lose her footing. She looks set to tumble into the vast abyss to the side of the catwalk but just manages to catch hold of the edge with one hand. The small BOX flies from her hand and hurtles down into the miles of blackness below. TIFFANY dangles over the edge, her feet kicking wildly for a foothold that doesn't exist.

Suddenly, a hand extends to her. She looks up. It is JULIA. For a second, nothing happens.

JULIA
Trust me.

TIFFANY lifts one hand off the edge and grabs at JULIA's proffered wrist.

JULIA begins to pull up and for a moment it seems the crisis is over. Then a terrible and familiar ripping noise is heard: The skin of the arm that TIFFANY clings to begins to rip free at the shoulder. Gradually, like a shirt's threads unraveling, it comes off. TIFFANY's weight pulls it clear like a very long and very tasteless evening glove and it seems she will finally make the long drop. At the final second, as the arm-skin comes off, the entire skin flies from the body and falls with its arm into the abyss. TIFFANY screams. She is going to die.

But suddenly the two arms that have Just lost their skin fly out again and catch her fingers. TIFFANY is hauled over the edge and staggers to her feet, staring into the-bloodied face of KIRSTY, who had donned JULIA's skin to help her friend.

The two girls share a quick and joyous embrace and then run rapidly up the catwalk. The camera stays with LEVIATHAN.

The rumbling stops. And the mountainous BOX creaks into its final, sealed position.

FADE OUT
FADE IN
INT. RECOVERY ROOM DAY
CLOSE UP on a bowl of beautiful flowers, sitting on a shelf in the recovery room.
The camera TRACKS out to let us see LARRY, pale, drawn, but basically okay, in the room's single bad. He is wired up to various drips and monitors.

Sunlight is flooding into the room from a window and the camera continues its TRACK
up to and through this window to;

EXT. HOSPITAL MAIN ENTRANCE DAY
KIRSTY is kissing TIFFANY on the cheek. TIFFANY is dressed in smart clothes and
has a small traveling bag in her hand.

KIRSTY
So. What're you going to do?
Open up a games-shop somewhere?
Sell jigsaw puzzles?
TIFFANY gives a smile.

TIFFANY
Oh, yeah.
There is a slightly awkward pause.

KIRSTY
Well ... G'bye.

TIFFANY
It's been Hell.
They share a rueful knowing smile, like the smile of soldiers back from a war who say
goodbye on a dockside and know they will never meet again.
TIFFANY turns and walks down the long path to the hospital gates.
KIRSTY watches her for a few moments and then turns and re-enters the institute.
The camera TRACKS back to the window of the RECOVERY ROOM and we watch
through the window as KIRSTY enters the room. She bends to kiss her father's cheek.
LARRY slips an arm around her shoulders and they embrace. The camera moves away
again.
122 INT. HALLWAY MALAHIDE's HOUSE DAY
The camera TRACKS slowly up MALAHIDE's hallway. The hallway is lined with
packing cases filled with items from the house. A
WORKMAN is shoving something into one of the cases. As the camera moves past
him, he speaks.

WORKMAN
So whose was all this shit?
The camera reaches the doorway of the OBSESSION ROOM as an answering voice is
heard.
2nd. WORKMAN
Not our problem...
The TRACK continues into -

INT. OBSESSION ROOM DAY

and we see the 2nd. WORKMAN. He is crouching over the mattress which is still in the middle of the floor of the otherwise empty room.

2nd. WORKMAN

... Gimme a hand with this.

Almost faster than the eye can register it, a hand shoots out from the mattress and grabs his wrist.

He has about half a second to issue a strangled shout and then, hideously quickly, a matter of two seconds or so, his body is drained of all life and the dried husk collapses to the floor.

The first WORKMAN appears hurriedly in the doorway and then freezes, an awestruck expression on his face.

JULIA is rising, headfirst and upright, from the centre of the mattress. The movement is smooth, magical, unsettling. It is graceful but not slow.

JULIA is fully fleshed, fully skinned, and fully dressed. She is in a replica of the dress MALAHIDE bought for her, but this one is jet black. She looks fabulous.

As the WORKMAN stands open-mouthed, her feet clear the mattress.

But they don't stop there. She slows to a graceful halt about six inches above the mattress. She stretches and flexes her arms sensually. Than her head swivels and her excited, aroused eyes meet those of the WORKMAN.

JULIA

I'm Julia. Love me.

Suddenly, her head tips back and, accompanied by JULIA's delighted laughter, a wide beam of Hell's black light flies at the ceiling from her open mouth. Instantaneously, it spills across the ceiling and falls,like a fountain of blood, across the screen.

www.ingramcontent.com/pod-product-compliance
Lightning Source LLC
Chambersburg PA
CBHW080915160726
48000CB00009B/2990